# Ethnicity and Biculturalism:
# Emerging Perspectives
# of Social Group Work

The *Social Work with Groups* series

# Ethnicity and Biculturalism: Emerging Perspectives of Social Group Work

Kenneth L. Chau
Editor

The Haworth Press
New York • London

*Ethnicity and Biculturalism: Emerging Perspectives of Social Group Work* has also been published as *Social Work with Groups*, Volume 13, Number 4 1990.

The Haworth Press, Inc., 10 Alice Street, Binghamton, NY 13904-1580
EUROSPAN/Haworth, 3 Henrietta Street, London WC2E 8LU England

**Library of Congress Cataloging-in-Publication Data**

Ethnicity and biculturalism: emerging perspectives of social group work / Kenneth L. Chau, editor

    p.  cm.

    "Has also been published as Social work with groups, Volume 13, Number 4, 1990" – T.p. verso.

    Includes bibliographical references.

    ISBN 1-56024-094-6 (H : acid free paper). – ISBN 1-56024-095-4 (pbk. : acid free paper)

    1. Social work with minorities. 2. Social group work. 3. Social service and race relations. 4. Biculturalism. I. Chau, Kenneth L.

HV3176.E835 1990

364.84'00973 – dc20

                                          90-47910

                                            CIP

# ABOUT THE EDITOR

**Kenneth L. Chau, PhD, MSW,** is Professor of Social Work at California State University at Long Beach. At the University, he chairs the Practice Sequence, is involved in developing a cross-cultural curricular focus for practice and research, and teaches in social work practice and research. Previously, Dr. Chau was Senior Lecturer in Social Work at the University of Hong Kong, where he taught for 12 years and engaged in developing cross-cultural training for graduate social work. Dr. Chau's current research and publications are in minority mental health, immigrant and refugee issues, and practice theory for cross-cultural clinical applications. Dr. Chau consults regularly on a broad range of issues involving ethnic minority populations locally and at the state level, and is a member of a task force on health and mental health of Southeast Asian refugees.

# Ethnicity and Biculturalism: Emerging Perspectives of Social Group Work

# Ethnicity and Biculturalism: Emerging Perspectives of Social Group Work

## CONTENTS

## What's New?                                         131

*Ruthann L. Rountree*

# Tributes
## to
## Beulah Rothman

## Founding Co-editor of *Social Work with Groups* 1924-1990

*London, England.* When the Editorial Board of *Groupwork* met recently, we felt great sadness that Beulah Rothman had died prematurely. She still had so much to do and to give. We are acutely aware of what a big loss her death will be to group work and groupworkers all over the world. To have lost such a warmhearted, enthusiastic and distinguished colleague must be a great blow.

We have always felt a special bond with our sister journal, *Social Work with Groups*. It has been a rich source of inspiration and encouragement in our own endeavours. We shall be publishing a tribute to Beulah Rothman in the next issue of *Groupwork*.

Allan Brown and Andrew Kerslake, Co-editors
David Whiting and Diana Birch, Publishers
All members of the Editorial Board of *Groupwork*

*West Hartford, Connecticut.* It is a chilly, windy October day in New England. There is a storm coming. The golden orange leaves fall from the trees. The green hang on. I am reading Katy's memoriam to Beulah. For the first time I can cry. Who can really believe Beulah is gone?

It is 1977, in a New York brownstone. There is a fast and strong dialogue going on about the formation of the Committee for the Advancement of Social Work with Groups. It sounds loud, angry. Beulah listens and then says, "Wait a minute. that's a crock. . ." She sits at the edge of her seat, her colorful scarf draping from shoulder to floor. Soon everyone is in on it. One would think the stakes were at least world peace! I remember disagreeing with her on a point but thinking, "Something very special has just happened here. This is quite a woman!" There are many of these meetings this year. This is my introduction to Beulah.

*xiii*

Beulah was always on the move and always in the midst of a small group, her arm over someone's shoulder. I remember a wonderful group meeting during a long car ride from the Baltimore Symposium in 1988. By the time we reached Beulah's drop-off-point we were a group with a long and close history. We laughed until we cried at Beulah's stories and jokes, and marveled at her sudden insights. A student remarked in amazement that she never dreamed she'd get to know a "group work legend."

Nor will I forget the ride from Connecticut to Flushing to deliver Beulah and Ivor to Katy's home before a Board meeting in New York. What a wonderful close time, made even closer as the group meeting continued. I left late at night with the feeling that it was premature to end the meeting. It was a feeling of loss.

There are too many moments to recall, some very close, some in disagreement, all in the context of love and respect. Perhaps the closest moments were at Beulah's home in Florida after George and I spoke at the Annual Conference of the Center for Group Work Studies. The subject was AIDS. Our discussion moved from issues of living and dying to living a life of difference. Beulah's gift to me was a very profound and special understanding and acceptance. She ended the discussion with "What difference is the difference?"

I loved Beulah. She was one of a kind. There is an empty seat at the head of the table that cannot be filled. It is premature to end the meeting.

Judith A.B. Lee, D.S.W.
University of Connecticut
President, Association for the Advancement
of Social Work with Groups

*Miami, Florida.* In 1981 I learned that Beulah Rothman was moving from New York to South Florida and would be joining my faculty to teach group work and direct the doctoral program. My feelings were excitement and mystery. I know and had taught many of Beulah's ideas through her writing, but now I would get to know her.

I did get to know Beulah Rothman. That is a privilege I will always treasure. I will note just a few things about what she was like as a colleague and what I learned from her. I found "mystery" to be important since I could never quite anticipate what I would be learning from Beulah.

Beulah was constantly creating groups. She had absolute integrity between her philosophy and her behavior. Courses were planned in groups. The Center for Group Work Studies was founded by a group. Lunchtime was a group event, during which two or three groups were being planned.

She was a master at honoring and using consensual, democratic processes and not permitting that process to lead to a mediocre decision or product.

She was comfortable with assertive use of power and did so, not for personal benefit, but to succeed with important ideas and programs.

The centerpiece of what I learned from Beulah, that I did not expect to learn, was about knowledge-building. She exemplified traditionalism in its most valuable form. In her writing, in her work for the journal, and in her work with AASWG, Beulah always considered two questions simultaneously: "Is it a treasured idea?" and "Does it fit with current reality?" She was not a historian for the sake of history. She was a historian to ensure that social group work's best ideas would not be lost, nor replaced by inferior ones.

I guess the other side of knowledge-building is knowledge-demolition. If that is so, Beulah would have been the one to chain herself to the doorway of a beautiful, still functional old building as the wrecking crew approaches. Who will take the role now that she is gone?

David F. Fike, PhD
Barry University School of Social Work

*Chapel Hill, North Carolina.* It was wonderful to have Beulah as a friend. She was always interested in what I was doing, how my health was, what was going on in my life—and I was grateful for her interest. It was a joy to see and talk with her at conferences.

Indirectly Beulah affected my life through her passionate devotion to the promotion of group work practice. She believed in the power of the group to enhance the lives of all and she fought to have this power recognized. She had strong convictions and she voiced them clearly. She knew that group work needed its advocates and she led the movement to advocate for it. She helped to found an avenue for ideas and she advanced the knowledge and careers of many a group work practitioner and educator, mine among them.

Maeda J. Galinsky, PhD
University of North Carolina
School of Social Work

*St. Louis, Missouri.* I too remember Beulah. I last saw Beulah in Montreal where we complained together about the injustices in the world. She was always sensitive to the plight of minorities and the poor, and adament that attention should be given to them by social workers, especially those who worked with groups. I always found support in expressing my concerns to Beulah. She too wanted to make changes occur in her lifetime.

Beulah my friend, I will miss your sincerity, your humor, and your strength.

Larry Davis, PhD
George Warren Brown School of Social Work
Washington University

# Preface

In the late 1930's and early 40's Kurt Lewin (1948) had a vision of the small group as a laboratory for developing democratic ideology and interpersonal behaviors, and for direct experience in group problem solving. Lewin saw the reality of the small group as a societal condition wherein the democratic ethos could be strengthened. So with our guest editor, Kenneth Chau, who clearly recognizes the power of the small group for fostering democratic attitudes and skills in the bicultural and multicultural society of the 90's.

When these editors first invited Ken Chau to take on the special editorship of this collection, we believed that the concern was for members of various cultural groups to be able to understand members of other groups, to live as neighbors in the dominant society without becoming alienated from the primary sources and to move comfortably within the polyglot world. Mass migrations of peoples across many borders, refugees straining legally and illegally toward a better life and neighborhoods receiving peoples of different colors, languages and religions in this and many western countries would certainly necessitate new levels of understanding and experience.

We had thought little about ethnic groups confronting each other in the interest of justice and identity. However, the new and dramatic spirit of glasnost suggests that we are living in a world that may be freer in one way but quite unskilled in bringing together ethnic differences, national aspirations and the struggle for peace in the world.

Group workers have no illusions that we can resolve the problems of society. But we do believe that what we bring to the human grouping process is one piece in the mosaic that can affect some people in becoming more universalistic and better able to reach out — unafraid of difference.

In this volume Ken Chau has been successful in assembling a group of authors who capture the full meaning of bicultural and multicultural understanding and association. We salute the writers of this collection of articles for their farsightedness in spotlighting a primary issue for this new decade. It occurs to us that Mary Follett (1934), a political scientist who greatly influenced group work in the post-WWI era, would cheer this volume as a confirmation and reaffirmation of her tireless activity in bringing people of all backgrounds together in "participatory democracy."

We are reminded too of the anthropologists' assertion (Kluckhohn and Kelly, 1945) that "every human is, in certain respects, (a) like all other humans, (b) like some other humans, and (c) like no other human" (degenderized by the writers). We suggest that this essential comment is an excellent starting point for a study of the content of this volume on social group work in a bicultural and multicultural mode.

We commend warmly Kenneth Chau and the authors of this volume. We find it gratifying that contemporary social group work efforts are so firmly rooted in the basics that were laid down by our visionary leaders of the past even as the present day realities are addressed with such creative professional skill.

*Catherine P. Papell*
*Beulah Rothman*

This volume was prepared and the Preface written before Beulah Rothman's death in August 1990.

## REFERENCES

Follett, Mary P. *The New State*. 4th Edition. New York: Longmans Greene and Co. 1934.

Kluckhohn, Clyde and Kelly, W.H. "The Concept of Culture" in *The Science of Man in the World Crisis*, edited by Ralph Linton. New York: Columbia University Press. 1945.

Lewin, Kurt. *Resolving Group Conflicts: Selected Papers on Group Dynamics*. New York: Harper. 1948.

# Foreword

Cultural diversity is a fact of life in the United States and in many other countries today, making it essential that social workers practice with sensitivity and competence to meet the needs and build on the strengths of the varied groups that comprise our population. That has always been a challenge, particularly for group work with its early history of serving immigrants and migrants within the context of their neighborhoods.

Grace Coyle's first book, *Social Process in Organized Groups* — published sixty years ago — is an example. She demonstrated how characteristics of the community milieu such as ethnic stereotypes, social class differences, dislocation of families, and the pluralistic nature of society affect individuals and the groups to which they belong. These themes persisted in her later writings. Another example is found in Gertrude Wilson and Gladys Ryland, *Social Group Work Practice*, 1949. They devoted considerable attention to race, religion, nationality, gender, and social class as factors of difference that influence group participation, citing many references on the subject. Several more recent books and numerous articles likewise attend to cultural factors in group composition, assessment of individuals and groups, and member-to-member relationships.

Margaret Hartford, in *Groups in Social Work*, reported numerous research studies on cultural factors in the formation of groups and in the development of interpersonal and intergroup relations. She noted that, for a period of many years, special efforts were made to include persons from various ethnic and racial backgrounds in both growth and task-oriented groups. Then, she said: "There followed a period of separation where identity with 'one's own kind' became a more popular issue, and group composition focused on single race, single ethnic, and to some degree, narrow range of socioeconomic levels" (p. 108). This change seemed to occur in re-

*xix*

sponse to growing ethnic awareness and recognition of the need to enhance positive ethnic identity. Now, a re-emerging trend is intensification of interest — not only in ethnic sensitive practice with single ethnic populations, but also in bicultural and multicultural practice, the subject of this publication. The ever-growing diversity of populations in our schools, work places, neighborhood facilities, and communities make it crucial for social workers to affirm ethnic identity and heritage, but simultaneously to promote intercultural acceptance and interdependence among group members. It may well be that the group is the modality of choice for enabling persons to acquire the essential attitudes, knowledge, and skills for living in a world characterized by racial, ethnic, religious, economic, and life-style diversity.

The collection of papers contained herein contributes greatly to these important interrelated purposes. The articles provide vivid descriptions of contemporary practice in various types of bicultural and multicultural groups, fields of practice, and countries. I began my own social work career in one of our most industrialized cities, characterized by serious conflicts between labor and management, unsavory environmental conditions, much poverty, and many still racially segregated facilities. Many opportunities were denied to the many poverty-stricken laborers, immigrants from Europe, and particularly to the growing number of black residents. One of my passions was to develop groups that would enhance interracial and intercultural acceptance and understanding, to de-segregate camps and other programs, and to fight with others to open up opportunities for the oppressed populations. We are still working on those matters today, but as the articles reveal, with much greater self-awareness, empathy, knowledge, and skills to bring to these tasks.

*Helen Northen, PhD*
*Emerita Professor of Social Work*
*University of Southern California*
*School of Social Work*

# Introduction:
# Facilitating Bicultural Development and Intercultural Skills in Ethnically Heterogenous Groups

## Kenneth L. Chau

As we enter into the 1990's, the demand for culturally competent practice—a legacy of the '80's fueled by demographic forces and a critical interest in ethnicity—will continue to shape the practice of social group work, especially as it involves people of diverse ethnic or racial backgrounds. The need for culturally competent group work is further illuminated by the emergence of a "new majority" in many states and by the growing diversity of our populations.

Early efforts have laid some important groundwork for making group work culturally relevant. These prior efforts have seen a turning point with the publication of a theme issue of this Journal—Ethnicity in Social Group Work Practice (Davis, 1984). That publication has put together outstanding works in group work practice with America's major ethnic minority groups. They introduce culturally compatible perspectives of group practice and provide knowledge and insights to guide the purpose and action of practitioners.

With the complex environments of the 1990's, however, the challenges that face group work practitioners are not simply one of strengthening ethnic identity. The multi-ethnic and multi-culturality of our society suggests that group work practice is more likely to be multi-ethnic than single-ethnic based. The goal of affirming ethnic

---

Kenneth L. Chau, PhD, is Professor of Social Work, California State University at Long Beach, 1250 Bellflower Boulevard, Long Beach, CA 90840-0902.

*1*

heritage and strengths will be useful if practitioners simultaneously enrich intercultural acceptance and interdependence among group members of differing ethnic cultures, including Euro-American ones. Being bicultural, i.e., possessing the ability to move freely between one's ethnic community and the larger culture, or being multicultural — having the attitudes, values, and skills to be competent among differing cultures, constitutes a primary goal towards which multi-ethnic group work should aim.

The authors in this volume affirm, in different ways, the need to address ethnicity and biculturalism simultaneously as practitioners respond to important issues in groups. These authors show how the practitioners must move back and forth between issues of culture congruence or difference on the one hand and the need for individual and social change on the other hand in ways that are culturally effective.

Lewis and Ford, for example, show how the concepts of ethnicity and biculturalism are intricately tied to intervention activities. The empowerment group work model that they present is for increasing utilization of social support networks in problem-solving with people of color. The group is a heterogeneous group of women, designed as an extension of groups commonly found in the members' personal and community environments and to demonstrate that changes that are expected to occur in a community must be developed in that community. In a similar manner, our British colleague Mullender demonstrates, through the Ebony Project, how groups for black children in white foster homes and also a group for the white foster carers can be assisted to deal with the challenges of newly found ethnicity and the impacts of racism in society or one's entrenched attitudes. These two articles have amply shown that tying ethnicity and biculturalism to the group plan, group leadership, group structure, group content, and group procedures in a thoughtful manner, it could certainly empower the individuals to take a fresh look at themselves and their own place in their environment.

The two articles by Bilides and Hurdle both look at groups composed of culturally diverse or multi-ethnic membership, but their treatment of the subject matter differ in approach and emphasis. Hurdle examines, for example, the interpersonal dynamics that operate in multi-ethnic groups and discusses three of Yalom's therapeutic factors in that context. Her thesis is that the meaning of these therapeutic factors may not be the same for members of ethnic and dominant groups because ethnic clients often experience therapeutic group differently. Bilides, on the other hand, focuses on issues of race, color, ethnicity, and class as they are played out in the group process of multi-ethnic, school-based, adolescent counseling groups. He notes that children of diverse backgrounds can learn about themselves and others from a group leader who is different from them and can also acquire enough confidence and understanding to be capable of moving freely between different cultures. To Bilides, the main challenge is to create an environment that is safe and accepting enough to allow these children to interact in new and positive ways. He offers some guidelines that should inform practitioners on managing diversity in groups and developing bicultural skills in group members. Both Bilides and Hurdle are confident that multi-ethnic groups will provide a human laboratory for learning about cultural differences and facilitating intercultural understanding and skills.

Multi-ethnic group work is not always restricted to a narrow treatment focus. This is borne out by Van Den Bergh's group use for a range of practice focus adapted from Chau's earlier work but applied to EAPs in academic settings, industries, and business sectors. She sees increased bicultural skills of the workforce, derived from self help and mutual aid of the group, as an asset to the employers as much as they are a benefit to the employees. In this as in other articles, a broad view of group practice is especially useful for tackling many unique concerns of ethnic minority people not otherwise considered in groups designed within a mainstream frame of reference.

In Anderson's article, for example, he offers a broad view of group work with families in Singapore, based on a multicultural perspective. The perspective is useful for understanding differing ethnic family groups (Chinese, Malay, Indian) experiencing cultural transition in terms of the family's cultural reality and value orientation. The variation in family culture and value orientation suggests a discriminative use of the group approach and making aspects of family culture, Anderson notes, the focus from which to begin any problem-solving process.

Chan's article highlights the differential use of single-session groups, supplemented by individualized services, as a possible means for facilitating cultural adaptation of Vietnamese refugees to the workforce and community life of Hong Kong. He describes the unique situations facing the refugee populations and the special programs implemented to help them develop bicultural skills.

In A Gaming Opportunity, we present three short pieces: Abels' The Basic Game, Glassman's Teaching Ethno-Racial Sensitivity through Groups, and Rountree's "What's New?" These are simulation games or structured exercises that have proven utility for the classroom or practice situations as a way to raise ethnic sensitivity, cultural self-awareness, and interracial understanding among the participants.

As a whole, the works included in this volume have addressed issues of ethnicity and biculturalism in group work practice in multicultural environments from a range of view points: that of direct service practitioners and social work educators; from coast to coast on our home ground and from far away but, nonetheless, intensely multicultural societies. We also see represented in these articles cultural diversity not confined only to ethnic minority groups. Of interest to note is that the majority of articles deal with groups composed of members coming from diverse ethnic backgrounds, and that practitioners of all the groups discussed here represent a different cultural background than the majority of their group members. This is truly reflective of the multicultural character of our society, one that is becoming rapidly the norm rather than the exception of our group membership and, perhaps to a lesser extent, of the group's leadership as well. This trend witnesses a shift toward an intercultural focus and it suggests important implications for social group work practice. First of all, we need to be able to plan our groups in a manner that incorporates cultural consideration systematically into every phase and all essential components of group work practice. There is a tremendous need for developing knowledge or familiarity into these areas. For example, we need to know what cultural factors are paramount in which phase of group development or which aspect of group practice. We also need to know when in the group process preoccupations with ethnicity should give way to consideration of other critical issues in group. Finally, in teaching group work practice, we need to give special effort to preparing students for the cultural dynamics of multi-ethnic groups, even if it means we must redefine what a traditional syllabus on group practice should cover.

This collection has provided practical insights and conceptual guidance into aspects of multi-ethnic group practice. Some inroads have been made, but our continued effort is needed if for no other reasons than to stand prepared for the challenges that our multicultural environments will present to group work practice in the 1990's.

## REFERENCES

Davis, Larry E. (1984). Ethnicity in Social Group Work Practice, Guest Editor, a special issue of *Social Work With Groups* 7(3).

# The Network Utilization Project: Incorporating Traditional Strengths of African-American Families into Group Work Practice

Edith A. Lewis
Briggett Ford

**SUMMARY.** This article outlines a model for ethnic and gender sensitive group work practice. It uses the preliminary results of an ongoing empowerment study with African-American mothers. Components and goals of the model are first presented. The initial implementation of the model and some of its outcomes (e.g., leader/member participation, group cohesion, empowerment, composition) are discussed. These outcomes are examined in terms of their implications for group work practice with other ethnic-group identified women of color.

## INTRODUCTION

Group work theory, practice and research have been traditionally devoted to the development of universal conceptualizations which can supposedly guide all group practice. This attention to standardizing methods has resulted in most researchers and practitioners ig-

Edith A. Lewis, MSW, PhD, is affiliated with the School of Social Work, 1065 Frieze Building, University of Michigan, Ann Arbor, MI 48109-2356. Briggett Ford, MSW, is affiliated with Community Casemanagement, Inc. Detroit, MI. The authors wish to thank the women who participated in this research and the community center staff who generously offered their support and assistance. We also express appreciation to Sandra Danziger and Daniel Steinmetz for their assistance in reading earlier versions of this manuscript.

noring the impact of member and leader ethnicity on group process
and outcomes (Sattler, 1977; Davis, 1979, 1980). The information
has generally flowed in one direction — from the wider society to the
communities of color in the United States. This has occurred largely
without concern for the conceptual or practice contributions to be
made by these communities.

Examples of these contributions are the existence and effective
operation of self-help and mutual aid groups which have supported
numerous communities populated primarily by ethnic groups of
color in the United States. Local church groups which developed in
a parallel fashion to group work practice in the United States (Quam
& Macht, 1986), and intervention groups serving some American
Indian nations (Edwards & Edwards, 1984) are included in this
number. Often the information about approaches which have been
found to be successful with populations of color have been dis-
missed because they have not emerged from the "mainstream"
helping professions. It has been posited that this is a result of the
few group practitioners, theorists and researchers of color (Davis,
1980; Lewis, 1988).

In turn, modern group work practice has been developed outside
of the traditional helping networks most ethnic groups in the United
States turn to when in trouble: family, friends, churches, neighbors,
respected community healers (Gutierrez, Ortega and Suarez, forthcoming). The result of this has been the development of the "artificial group"; one generally meeting outside the community of origin
for the members, ignores their bicultural status, and which substi-
tutes for traditional helping networks of its constituents. Often, the
member must choose between the norms of the group versus the
norms of the community of origin, thus compounding the existing
tension between these forces and impeding personal growth. It is
possible that the lack of participation in these "artificial groups" by
people of color is a result of their structure and operation outside of
their communities.

Gender also plays a significant role in group process and outcome
(Althof and Keller, 1980; Dion, 1985). Gender influences affect
participant/leader interactions, group composition issues, the development of group cohesion, and goal attainment. One of the criti-

cisms of work which only incorporates one view of the construct of gender, however, is that it gives "voice" to only one portion of the phenomenon. Thus, it does not acknowledge the possibility of different constructs of gender, each related to important variables such as the ethnicity and class of the group member (Kissman and Lewis,1989; Adams-Sawyer et al., 1986; Baca-Zinn et al., 1986). It is widely agreed that to work effectively with women of color, one must understand their bicultural experiences; those shaped by interaction with the wider society and by the community of color (Gutierrez, 1988; Lewis, 1989; Gutierrez and Lewis, in press). Groups designed for women which assume one universal view of the world have not been successful for women of color any more than universal groups have worked for people of color in general.

What, then, are some of the potentially combined effects of ethnicity, bicultural status, and gender on important group work practice concerns? In what ways might leader/member interaction be affected by the groups' perception of the leader's race? In what ways does a group's ethnic composition affect its members' ability to self-disclose? In what ways may self-help groups provide practice knowledge regarding the issues of ethnic homogeneity versus heterogeneity? Do these groups provide information on possible measure of group cohesion? Further, is it possible to design group interventions which consider ethnicity, the bicultural status of women of color and their perceptions of gender together as important variables?

This article examines these issues in the context of an ongoing study of an empowerment group work model with African-American mothers. The model was specifically designed to be used with women from ethnic groups of color, whose bicultural status provides two sets of behavioral options: one within their communities of origin and another within the wider society. It was hoped that the Network Uilitzation Project could provide a strategy for making decisions about the efficacy of particular behavioral options for women of color.

The components and goals of the Network Utilization Project (NUP) model are first presented, along with a description of weekly sessions and homework. Next, the implementation results are described in terms of the group measures listed above. Finally, the outcomes are discussed in terms of their implications for group work practice with other ethnic group-identified women of color.

## THE MODEL

The Network Utilization Project (NUP) is based on the developmental research strategy of Thomas (1984), and was designed for group work with women of color. It strategically and purposefully incorporates strengths of African-American communities (Aschenbrenner, 1979; Billingsley, 1968; Hill, 1971). The major assumption of the NUP model is that people work most effectively when they are in groups which they consider to be very similar to those that are part of their natural environments. One of our goals is to create intervention environments that are perceived to be extensions of daily personal and community environments (Davis, 1984). In other words, we have tried, through NUP to acknowledge the bicultural nature of ethnic group membership, and the existence of informal and formal community of color structures (Billingsley, 1968; Lewis and Kissman, 1990).

A major objective of the Network Utilization Project is to empower African-American women by increasing their systematic use of social support networks in resolving individual and community problems. We attempt in NUP to build upon the strengths of traditional family, friend, partner and religious networks in the lives of African-American women (Lewis, 1989; Manns, 1981; McAdoo, 1981, 1983). Emphasis is placed, then, on the use of existing social networks for problem resolution, and on the purposeful creation of new ones. The model includes elements of cognitive and behavioral interventions including the functional analysis of behavior (Turner, 1982; Mitchell-Jackson, 1982), systematic desensitization (Wolpe, 1982), rational behavior therapy (Maultsby, 1984), stress innoculation (Meichenbaum, 1985), and personal science (Mahoney, 1977). These assessment and intervention techniques were integrated into a set of procedures with seven components: a focus on individual and community problems, a focus on the small group, the group environment, weekly sessions and homework, and a focus on written and graphic instruments.

## 1., 2. Focus on Individual and Community Problems

The initial structure of the model included separate components focusing on individual and community problems. We initially believed that the group members would work in a group setting on individual problem resolution for a period of eight weeks and then, having established a pattern of interaction within the group, be able to work cooperatively on analysis and resolution of a community concern. Unlike other group interventions, the empowerment emphasis of the project requires that identification of the problems to be resolved are determined by the group members (Solomon, 1976; Swift and Levin, 1987).

The concepts of "community" must also be constructed by the group members, a factor sometimes ignored in group composition. Understanding the perceptions of bicultural women about their community as well as ethnic group membership is essential. For example, the term community may refer to a geographic locality or a psychological bond with a group of people, as in the case of the different uses of the term "The Black Community" by African-Americans. In the same vein, the term Native Americans masks the different tribes included in the umbrella, each with different experiences in the U.S. and different current statuses within the wider society (Gutierrez and Lewis, in press).

## 3. Small Group Setting

The third major component of the model is a focus on the small group setting. A maximum of ten members were allowed, so that an optimum group size of eight would be anticipated at group sessions. The only restrictions placed on the group were that those members agreeing to participate would be available for both the individual and community components of the program, and would attempt homework assignments. The group was also structured with two African-American women co-facilitators, for several reasons. The importance of considering leader/participant similarities in group work practice has been well documented (Davis, 1981; Rose, 1977; Chu and Sue, 1984). Strategically placing same ethnic-group and gender members in the facilitator roles of the groups increased the ability to role model techniques. It was also helpful to have two recorders to increase the validity of process recordings collected during the group sessions.

### 4. Session Environment

NUP focuses, also, on the environment in which the sessions are to be conducted. We assume that changes which are expected to be demonstrated in a community must be developed in that community. Therefore, this model has been designed for use in a neighborhood community center, church, or other natural setting. This allows participants to retain some of the sense of connection with their natural environment, thereby increasing the probability of cohesion within the group, and achievement of individual and group objectives. It further focuses on one of the basic tenets of empowerment — that of assisting people to act upon their increased perceptions of self-efficacy (Gutierrez, 1988).

### 5. Focus on Weekly Sessions

A fifth component of the model is the format which emphasizes weekly sessions of at least two hours' duration. This weekly interaction provides opportunities for the facilitators and group members to reinforce applications of the behavioral techniques utilized by group members and to refine programmatic objectives in a timely fashion. Another advantage of the weekly sessions is that they allow the women to practice providing mutual support to each other in the group which can be generalized to their other interactions in the community during the remainder of the week.

### 6. Weekly Homework

The sixth component of the project is the assignment of weekly homework. Here the goal is again a chance to practice gains made through the group in the person's natural environment. Weekly homework gives the women some feeling of control over the changes that they are making in their lives because it allows them to modify techniques learned in the group sessions to the realities of their individual and family experiences. The homework also gives participants a concrete gauge of the changes they are making and the results of these changes on other members of their social networks. This also helps to create a sense of investment in the group as the homework is reported on at the beginning of each session and helps to determine the agenda of each meeting.

## 7. Focus on Written and Graphic Instruments

Use of written and graphic instruments to inform individual and community change are the final, and most complex, component of the NUP model. Each problem identified by group members is submitted to four-stage analysis process. (A) In the first stage, a range of problems affecting the individual or community are generated. These problems are then prioritized in terms of their severity to the individual or group. The most important of these problems is then expanded so that it can be described in measurable and objective terms which can be understood by the entire group.

(B) Secondly, the target problem is subjected to a thorough task-analysis, as group members write down all of the ideas they can generate about the "action steps" required to resolve their identified problem. This is first done on an individual basis, but returned to in later weeks as a group exercise with the task analysis being modified as changes are made in the target problem resolution plan.

(C) Most importantly in this project, group members participate in a network analysis (Atteneave, 1969) which lists the names of people available to assist them. Five major categories of people are listed: family, friends, church members, partners, and "others." Families include any person the individual cares to list as a family member, and listing extended family or fictive kin members is encouraged. Instructions for the listing of partners includes current romantic relationships, irrespective of marital status or sex of the individual. Lastly, the category of "others" includes any significant relationship to the individual. This could include teachers, social service personnel, counselors, or landlords, among others.

(D) After completing the network analysis, group members return to their target problems and eliminate any persons listed on the network who would not be available to assist them in the problem resolution. This is a critical step in the model as it is necessary to clarify that everyone in the network may not be suitable for involvement in every problem encountered by the individual. The literature on social network utilization has noted that some network members work in opposition to the growth of particular members and that African-American women who, because of their ethnic group membership, have a higher probability of being a part of an extended network than women from most European ethnic group backgrounds, must be careful to examine their networks for potential "saboteurs" to their continued growth (Lewis, 1988; McAdoo, 1983).

This process of elimination consists of an exercise listing the "pros and cons" of asking each individual member of the network for assistance with the target problem. When members are eliminated from the list, there is a conscious acknowledgement that they are not eliminated from the social network and that they must be considered as being potentially impacted by the problem resolution strategies.

Once the new, target-problem-specific-network has been established, participants engage in a process of identifying strategies to engage members of that network to help. Practice of these strategies and ideas for others are generated within the group. These strategies form the basis of the intervention plan. Each week, group members choose a portion of their individual problem-solution plans to work on, report findings of earlier attempts back to the group, modify their plans and practice skills related to operationalizing the plan. Their instruments describing the goal, objective, task analysis, beginning and ending networks are kept together in a notebook to which they can refer through the group experience.

While detailed, the NUP model is an easily administered project which can use the bicultural natural environment to help participants generate individual and community change. Selected outcomes of the initial administration of the model are reported in the next section.

## THE IMPLEMENTATION PROCESS

A group based on this model was formed in the winter and spring of 1988 in a midwestern city and resulted in some interesting group process and outcome findings. Specifically, change was identified with regard to the empowerment of members, the maintenance of cohesion within and outside the physical group, and the interaction between group members and leaders. Each of these areas are discussed in this section.

The gains made by group members in the Network Utilization Project's measures of empowerment were dramatic. Their ability to analyze community and individual problems and solutions within and outside the group increased. More importantly, however, was their increased ability to act on the new information to change their environments. Within the group, each member had chosen at least one problem for individual behavioral change. Of the 10 members of the group, 8 either met their goal or made significant progress toward it. Among the changes were the perceived support of members while they engaged in such efforts as appealing a grant-denial from the local and regional Departments of Social Services, appealing an order to remove a husband from a family by the judicial system, the filing of an aging, disabled woman for benefits under the OASDHI program, and informally removing two unruly stepchildren from a group member's home. Moreover, individual target problem change did not end with the termination of the group in the late spring of 1988. Participants continued to work on initially listed problems.

Community changes growing out of the group were equally impressive. Participants formed a tenant's organization that successfully lobbied the local City Council to deny funding to an agency which had a long history of receiving payment for services in the low-income community which it did not provide. Plans for the formation of the tenant's organization as well as activities related to the campaign to oust the agency were developed by and practiced in the group.

It is important to return to the concept of community discussed earlier in this article. While the agency was geographically located within the physical boundaries of the community, over time, community residents did not perceive it to be responsive to their needs or as having an interest in their welfare. The agency had long since stopped being perceived as a community agency and was, instead, viewed as an unwelcome imposer of the needs of the wider society on the predominantely African-American community. This difference in perception made it less difficult for the residents to lobby to close the agency.

An unanticipated outcome of group support was the community's response to the group's existence. The group began to serve as a new vehicle for the mutual support and aid of members. On several occasions, family members of group participants approached the group sessions to ask for emotional or physical assistance for their kin. Other community members also approached the group for assistance in resolving their individual or social service concerns.

Sensitivity to the possibility of different constructs of gender within the ethnic community led to interesting results. While the focus of the group was on the women in the community, it did not seek to do so at the expense of the men. On several occasions, men came in contact with the group and viewed it as an important part of the community. Only on one occasion did a man question the existence of the group, and then only did so on the grounds that there was no men's counterpart in the community. This strategy differs from the stance of other community-based group programs which seek to work only with the women, and thereby removing themselves from positive contacts with the entire community.

The group later identified the need to link with other low-income communities and ethnic groups of color in the city to coordinate service provision. While the actual management of the emerging city-wide low-income tenant's rights organization was done outside of the group, discussions of its necessity were initiated within the group and its leadership was composed of group members.

A follow-up of group activities in the winter of 1989-90 found some group members, through their Tenant's Council, had successfully defeated an attempt by the city's administration to close down their entire housing project and relocate the residents. Residents had requested to be moved only to safe and affordable housing, and when that could not be guaranteed, launched a protest in the city, using the tools of interacting with the wider society through lobbying and media attention initially role-played in the group setting.

There were predictable and unpredictable outcomes with respect to the interaction between group members and leaders. Knowledge of the history of African-Americans and racial dynamics are essential in group work (Davis, 1984) and we incorporated these into the development and processes of the group. For example, prior to the group's initial meeting, one of the facilitators spent six months in the community working with a children's program and meeting community residents. Group participants later reported that their interest in participating in the group stemmed from their observance of the facilitator's work with their children. Understanding the "children as wealth" hypothesis which operates in many African-American communities (McAdoo, 1982) was beneficial in the initiation of the NUP model. It is important to note that entry into the community was facilitated by the leader's prior work in the community. While this is desirable, it is unclear that it is necessary.

Role assignments affected group member and facilitator interaction patterns. One physically younger and less experienced facilitator was viewed as a peripheral member, as evidenced by the limited number of interactions directed toward her by group members. This was due, in part, to the limited responsibility given her for initiating group discussions and activities. Her contributions to the group were valuable to role model behavior and provide process recordings of the sessions.

The other facilitator was alternately viewed as peer and expert by group members. This is best illustrated by an incident in which one of the group members, in modifying her task analysis, added the name of the facilitator and her professional title. She had not used the title before in referring to the facilitator and, when questioned about it, replied that she was referring to the expert role the facilitator had demonstrated in another incident affecting a group member.

Although the Network Utilization Project was designed specifically for African-American women, two of the ten initial participants were white, resulting in a racially heterogenous group. The white women were both from Appalachian backgrounds and had lived in the geographically and economically segregated community for several years; thus were known to the community residents.

Ethnicity was raised as a variable in the initial group session as the group process, goals and objectives were explained to potential members. Group norms were developed that did not denigrate group members because of their ethnic backgrounds and these were adhered to by participants throughout the project. Ethnicity was raised again on a number of occasions, however, as group members talked about problems arising from how their individual and familial values differed from those in the wider society. We believe that these deliberate discussions and attention to members' ethnic and racial backgrounds highlighted members' awareness of their bicultural status. More importantly, however, we believe that this attention stressed the legitimacy of options based on the norms of the community of color. Group norms specified that ethnic differences would not be translated as ethnic deficiencies. African-American group members viewed the Appalachian-reared women as more alike than unlike them on most issues arising in the group.

This heterogeneity did not have a visible effect on individual self-disclosure in the group. Most participants irrespective of ethnic group membership, felt free to reveal intimate details of their lives which had been previously unknown to their neighbors and, in some cases, even family members. Again, modelling of self-disclosing statements by facilitators who gave examples of their own attempts to use the strategies employed in the group assisted group members in verbally expressing their concerns about themselves and their community. One illustration of this surrounded child-rearing practices. The facilitator with children at home shared the dilemma of using different types of punishment with her children. The options of using spanking (considered an acceptable option among many African-American extended families) and time out (a strategy often taught to parents in the wider society) were compared. The benefits and drawbacks of both strategies were contrasted, such as the potential for the family to be reported to Protective Services in the case of the use of the former strategy. Explicit attention to the differences in strategy and differences in community and wider society expectations about appropriate behavior served as a model for future discussions in the group.

There was, however, one marked exception, a group member who remained silent through the first ten weeks of the project while, actively engaging in the written and new skill acquisition activities of the group. She only began to talk about her individual intervention in the last third of the project. At the same time, she became quite assertive with family members and friends who had previously come to expect her silence and were surprised by the change.

## IMPLICATIONS FOR SOCIAL GROUP WORK PRACTICE

Outcomes described in this paper suggest that an ethnic-sensitive model of group work which focuses on the bicultural status and existing strengths of the population of color has merit. Important factors such as the need for the group leader to be well-acquainted with community norms and potential participants, the wisdom of housing the intervention group within the community that change is expected to take place, the conscious and consistent discussion of ethnicity in any heterogenous group and the reinforcement of individual and community attempts at empowerment must be considered in work with populations of color. This ethnic and gender-sensitive model of group work practice with its emphasis on raising ethnicity, race and bicultural status of the populations of color involved as ongoing issues in the group also has merit for ethnically heterogenous groups.

A discussion of the common concerns shared by the women in the community allowed for the development of a common conceptualization of gender—a common "lens" with which to link the intervention. This lens did not link the members to all women, but did allow for them to see similarities with other women in similar life circumstances, irrespective of their ethnic and, potentially in the case of the facilitators, class backgrounds.

These preliminary findings must be taken with some caution, however. The intervention model was implemented primarily with African-American women and is not generalizable to all populations of color due to the potentially different norms associated with different ethnic group membership. For example, facilitators insisting upon maintaining a peer/expert role in group process may find that strategy ineffective for some Asian/Pacific Islander populations who are more comfortable with the facilitator-as-expert role in intervention (Ho, 1984).

Revisions in the model are being made, such as true co-facilitation of all aspects of the project, so that participants do not rely solely on one group facilitator. Individual and group components of the program, conceptually separated in the initial model, have been merged so that individual and community problems may be worked on simultaneously. Further development, refinement and administration of the model is being undertaken to examine its efficacy across as well as within ethnic and gender groups.

In sum, the Network Utilization Project model has the potential for increasing utilization of social work interventions with populations of color. It is an extension of the concept of biculturalism in communities of color, exists in concert with these populations of color, and attempts to empower individuals to perceive themselves as effective change agents and to act upon these perceptions. The model serves as an example of the contributions communities of color have to make to social group work practice when the flow of information is bi-directional, from the community of color to the wider society; that is, when biculturalism truly informs practice. As the number and proportion of persons of color in the United States increases during the next decade, it is crucial that practice methods, and particularly group practice methods, are made more ethnic and gender sensitive.

## REFERENCES

Adams-Sawyer, Z., Adams-Sullivan, M., Brown-Manning, R.B., DeLaCruz, A.C., & Gaines, E. Women of color and feminist practice. In Brinker-Jenkins, M. and Hooyman, N. (Eds.) *Not For Women Only: Social Work Practice For A Feminist Future*. Silver Spring, MD: NASW, 1986.

Althof, S.E., and Keller, A.C. Group therapy with gender identity patients. *International Journal of Group Psychotherapy*, 1980, 30, 481-490.

Aschenbrenner, J. Continuities and variations in Black family structure. In Shimkin, D.B., Shimkin, E.M., & Frote, D.A. (Eds.) *The Extended Family in Black Societies*. Paris: Mouton Publishers, 1978, 181-200.

Attneave, C. Therapy in tribal settings and urban network utilization. *Family Process*, 1969, 8, 192-210.

Baca-Zinn, M., Cannon, L.W., Higgenbotham, E., and Dill, B. The costs of exclusionary practices in women's studies. *Signs*, 1986, 11 (2), 290-303.

Billingsley, A. *Black Families in White America*. Englewood Cliffs, N.J.: Prentice-Hall, 1968.

Chu, J., and Sue, S. Asian/Pacific-Americans and group practice. *Social Work With Groups*, 1984, 7 (3), 23-35.

Davis, L.E. Racial composition of groups, *Social Work*, 1979, 24, 208-213.

Davis, L.E. Racial balance: A psychological issue. *Social Work With Groups*, 1980, 3 (2), 75-85.

Davis, L.E. Racial issues in the training of group workers. *Journal for Specialists in Group Work*, August, 1981, 155-160.

Davis, L.E. Essential components of group work with Black Americans. *Social Work With Groups*, 1984, 7 (3), 97-109.

Dion, K.L. Sex, gender and groups: Selected issues. In O'Leary, V, Unger, R., and Wallston, B. (Eds.) *Women, Gender and Society*. Hillsdale, N.J.: Erlbaum, 1985.

Edwards, E.D., and Edwards, M.E. Group work practice with American Indians. *Social Work With Groups*, 7 (3), 1984, 7-21.

Gutierrez, L. Working With Women of Color: An Empowerment Perspective. Paper presented at the National Association of Social Workers Annual Conference "Choices and Challenges," Philadelphia, PA, November, 1988.

Gutierrez, L., and Lewis, E. Feminist Organizing With Women of Color. In Erlich, J. & Rivera, R. *Community Organizing With People of Color* (in press).

Gutierrez, L., Ortega, R., and Suarez, Z. Self help and the Latino community. In Powell, T. (Ed.) *Working with Self Help*. Silver Spring, MD: NASW (forthcoming).

Hill, R. *Strengths of Black Families*. Washington, D.C.: National Urban League, 1971.

Kissman, K., and Lewis, E. Ethnic-Sensitive Feminist Social Work Practice. Working Paper Series, School of Social Work, University of Michigan, Ann Arbor, MI, 1989.

Lewis, E. Role strengths and strains of African-American mothers. *Journal of Primary Prevention*, 9 (1&2), Fall/Winter, 1988, 77-91.

Lewis, E. Role strain in Black women: The efficacy of social networks. *Journal of Black Studies*, in press.

Lewis, E. and Kissman, K. Factors in Ethnic-Sensitive Feminist Social Work Practice. *Arete*, 14 (2), Winter, 1989.

Macht, M., and Quam, J. *Social Work: An Introduction*. Columbus, Ohio: Merill, 1986.

Mahoney, M.J. Some applied issues in self-monitoring. In Cone, J., and Hawkins, R. (Eds.) *Behavioral Assessment: New Directions in Clinical Psychology*. New York: Brunner/Mazel, 1977.

Manns, W. Support systems of significant others in Black families. In McAdoo, H. (Ed.) *Black Families*. Beverly Hills: Sage, 1981, 238-251.

Maultsby, R.C. *Rational Behavior Therapy*. Englewood Cliffs, N.J.: Prentice-Hall, 1984.

McAdoo, H.P. Patterns of upward mobility in Black families. In McAdoo, H.P. (Ed.) *Black Families*. Beverly Hills: Sage, 1981, 155-179.

McAdoo, H.P. Demographic trends for people of color. *Social Work*, 27 (1). 1982, 15-23.

McAdoo, H.P. Work roles and coping strategies of employed single Afro-American mothers. Paper presented at the National Council on Family Relations Annual Meeting, St. Paul, Minnesota, October 13, 1983.

Meichenbaum, D.H. *Stress Inoculation Training*. New York: Pergamon Press, 1985.

Mitchell-Jackson, A. Psychosocial aspects of the therapeutic process. In Turner, S., and Jones, R. (Eds.) *Behavior Modification in Black Populations*. New York: Plenum Press, 1982, 21-38.

Rose, S.D. *Group Therapy: A Behavioral Approach*. Englewood Cliffs, N.J.: Prentice Hall, 1977.

Sattler, J.M. The effects of therapist-client racial similarity. In Gurman, A., and Razdin (Eds.) *Effective Psychotherapy: A Handbook of Assessment*. New York: Pergamon Press, 1977, 252-290.

Solomon, B. *Black Empowerment*. New York: Columbia University Press, 1976.

Swift, C., and Levin, G. Empowerment: An emerging mental health technology. *Journal of Primary Prevention*, 8 (1&2), Fall/Winter, 1987, 71-94.

Thomas, E. *Designing Intervention for the Helping Professions*. Beverly Hills: Sage, 1984.

Turner, S.M. *Behavior modification and Black populations*. In Turner, S. and Jones, R. (Eds.) *Behavior Modification In Black Populations*. New York: Plenum Press, 1982, 1-19.

Wolpe, J. *The Practice of Behavior Therapy* (3rd Ed.) New York: Pergamon Press, 1982.

# The Ebony Project —
# Bicultural Group Work
# with Transracial Foster Parents

Audrey Mullender

**SUMMARY.** The project encompassed groups for black children in white foster homes and also a group for the white carers, which forms the main topic of this paper. The group aimed to assist the carers to consider what special needs their foster children had, as well as challenging their understanding of the impact of racism in society and of their own assumptions. The ethnicity of group workers, the consultant and of other agency staff were all highly relevant to the success of the group and to the particular difficulties it encountered. The bicultural worker team was especially valuable in confronting the defensive attitudes which prevailed amongst group members. The Ebony project demonstrates the potential for innovative group work practitioners to redress the failings of a past era when ethnicity was frequently simply ignored and when the needs of service users were consequently not appropriately met.

In recent months, the fierce debate over whether transracial placements can ever fully meet the needs of black children has once again captured the attention of British journalists, both in the social work press and in the popular daily newspapers. Headlines in the latter have screamed hatred at social workers who, it is alleged, have dragged black children away from their white foster parents

Audrey Mullender, MA, is Lecturer in Social Work at the University of Nottingham, England. She holds a BA in French, an MA in Social Work and the Certificate of Qualification in Social Work. She was Consultant to the Ebony foster carers' group (which forms the major topic of this paper) and has had sixteen years' experience of practice, teaching and research in the fields of child care and of group work.

23

for no other reason than their rigid and mistaken belief that only black or mixed race couples can bring them up adequately. Debates around ethnicity do not come any more polarized or voluble than this one.

Two or three particular cases have caused this renewed outcry. Reporting restrictions make it extremely hard to know exactly what has transpired, except that the Courts have subsequently backed social work decisions in the most widely reported instance. Word on the professional grapevine suggests that, in addition to the usual complex and intertwined multiplicity of factors affecting the life of any child in foster care, there have been problems in some long-established transracial foster families in tolerating access by the children's birth relatives (Loftus, 1986) or co-operating with plans to return children to their black families of origin. With racial discrimination still very strong at many levels of British society, it is often easier for people to accept an attractive black child into their home (and probably, thereafter, to raise them as if they were white), than to confront all the prejudicial feelings and attitudes raised by contact with black adults and the reality of the child's future as a black member of a predominantly white, racist society.

This is not the first period in recent history when social workers in this country have encountered such adverse publicity. The issues were equally live in the early to mid-1980's and indeed, underlay the development of the Ebony project, which forms the subject of this paper. One of the aims of the project was to recognise the responsibility of agencies to work more appropriately with their transracial foster carers, rather than turning their backs on families who, after all, had been recruited and selected by them in the first place. Since that time, the project has remained unique in British social work, firstly because of its attempt to raise the quality of long-standing transracial placements and, secondly, owing to its use of group work as the major method of intervention. Nevertheless, the lessons from the project are of far wider applicability. The whole of professional practice and training in this country urgently needs to respond to the imperatives of race and the development of anti-racist working (CCETSW,1989). The Ebony workers showed that this can be done, even in a context of hitherto unquestioning and unchallenged practice. They also demonstrated the value of group work in this regard.

## THE EBONY PROJECT

Black social workers in Nottingham, in the East Midlands area of England, have led the way in their agency's commitment both to reducing the disproportionate numbers of black children removed from their families and to increasing the number of same-race placements for those children who continue to be so removed. A further practice concern, however, has been to meet the needs of those children and young people who are already settled in white homes and who, as a consequence, may be feeling confused about their identity, flattened by the racially motivated name-calling and other abuse which a white background has not given them the skills or the composure to handle, and generally lacking in self-confidence.

Whilst a growing number of black social workers in Britain and an occasional black psychologist (Maxime, 1987) have worked with individual children to increase their knowledge of their cultural heritage and to improve their self-esteem, the Ebony project—encompassing groups for transracially placed children and one group to date for their white foster carers (our particular concern in the paper which follows)—represents the only group work response of which the present author is aware. As such, it has raised particular questions about the ways in which bringing people together in groups can help them to reflect more widely on their own situation, see the world through others' eyes and, it is hoped, eventually change their own attitudes and behaviour. These benefits of group membership will be illustrated in the body of this paper.

## THE FIRST EBONY GROUP

The initial Ebony Group, for Afro-Caribbean (including mixed parentage) children living in white foster families, ran in 1983 (Miller, 1985; Mullender and Miller, 1985). A black student from the University of Nottingham, then on her practice placement, was asked if she could undertake some personal identity counselling with a black child who was fostered long term, in a stable transracial placement, but who seemed to be rather depressed. The student, Doreen Miller, suspected that the problem stemmed from the young person's discomfort or lack of support in his white family and felt sure that there were others in the same situation. She decided to bring them together by running a group.

She found two other black workers to be her co-leaders, and asked social workers to refer to her any black children on their caseloads who lived in white families and who could benefit from attending a group during the summer vacation. The general aims of the group were:

1. to give members a positive experience of black adults as role models,
2. to help the children begin to establish friendships with other young black people in a similar position to themselves,
3. to inform the children about the positive contributions that black people in the past and present have made to British society,
4. to develop their self-esteem through this experience,
5. to acquaint the black children, many of whom lived in isolated, rural communities, with the realities of being black— including racism and discrimination—and to help them develop skills in dealing with these.

The group was given the name 'Ebony' by its members, who felt the term conveyed a positive image of blackness. Leading members of the local black community volunteered their time to lead group sessions on the following topics:

— History of the Caribbean
— Hair and skin care
— Black people in history
— Caribbean food
— Language and dialect
— Black music

The positive features of the first Ebony young people's group were repeated the second time it ran, when most of the group enjoyed the sessions and would have welcomed the chance to attend a similar group again. Some of the children became interested enough to go off to the library and borrow books on West Indian history. The appearance of many of the group members changed. They became smarter and brighter in dress and appearance. Many members were able to share openly some of the painful experiences of racism they had undergone, and their previous denial of their identity.

In order to follow up some of the issues from the first Ebony group with the young people's foster carers, a joint session was held at the end of the group. Only one couple came to this meeting. They had seen little point in the group because they perceived no problems for black youngsters growing up in white families; as they put it, "We're all God's children." They also could not see anything wrong in telling their foster child the rhyme "When God made little nigger boys," despite the fact that it used racist language and also seemed to accord black children very much a secondary status. It seemed important that future Ebony groups should find ways of involving foster carers more fully in the overall aims of the Ebony project. Consequently, when a second Ebony Group was run, in 1985/6, a group for the young people's carers was run in parallel with it.

## FOSTER CARERS' GROUP

Recruitment to the foster carers' group was essentially linked to the decision as to who to invite to the young people's group since it was intended that they would come from the same families and that the groups would meet in parallel. Despite initial agreements to come along, in the event, attendance at the group was neither as high nor as consistent as had been hoped. Some group members dropped out while the group was still running, including one couple who continued to take their foster children along to the young people's group after they had themselves ceased attending the carers' group. The core membership settled at about four or five at each meeting.

For this and other reasons, the group was not an easy experience for the leaders who had to work very hard with a consultant to keep up their own morale and sense of direction. The prevailing tensions nationally, against which backdrop the group took place (referred to in the introduction to this paper), reflected opposing voices; one side attacking transracial placements as inevitably unable to meet the particular needs of black children or the wishes of the black community, and the other arguing that they were often the only alternative to children languishing in residential care for long periods and could, in any case, provide very good homes. The group workers were firm supporters of same-race placements, and of recruiting additional black families to make these a reality, but also felt that the agency had a responsibility to make its existing transracial placements as good as possible, however hard this might be at this rather belated stage.

The aims of the group were specifically geared, therefore, towards those areas of the children's needs which resulted directly from their ethnicity and which, it was felt by the agency, the foster carers had been meeting least well. The establishment of the group represented a decision by the agency to take a large degree of the responsibility for this past failure to respond to all the children's needs. After all, whereas more general matters involved in the preparation and training of foster carers had been or were being dealt with in other forums, the group leaders did not feel that the transcultural nature of these placements had really been tackled at all. Whilst this would necessarily result in a challenging style of group work, they felt they owed it to the foster carers to make good this deficit.

The precise aims of the foster carers' group were:

1. to provide opportunities for white foster carers of black children to share experiences, problematic or otherwise, arising from the transcultural nature of the placements.
2. to act as a training resource covering any special physical and emotional needs of black children in foster care;
3. to try and move the foster carers toward a more culturally aware parenting style;
4. to offer carers a model of the survival skills which a black child needs in present-day British society, given that racism is never far below the surface.

These aims reflect the need to move away from the complacency of doing nothing different for black children in foster care than for their white counterparts. They also mean going beyond the typical first reaction of white carers who begin to realize that their black foster children *do* have particular needs which they might wish to learn more about — the classically safe issues of hair and skin care — into the more fraught areas of racial identity, the ability to survive in a racist society, and the added difficulties which transracial foster parents find in dealing with these.

In addition to setting the aims for the group, the workers were concerned to consider a range of other issues which had a bearing on the ethnically sensitive material which the group would be tackling. The ethnic origin of the group leaders and of their consultant was an obvious starting point for these discussions. The eventual decision was that the leadership team should be bicultural in make-up, thus reflecting the bicultural nature both of the wider society and of the families participating in the project. A black consultant was unfortunately not available, so the present author played that role and attempted not to subvert or block any of the issues which the black leaders, particularly, felt were essential in the group's content and functioning. The relevance of the ethnicity of other members of staff in the agency also became apparent as the group progressed, particularly the gaps in the support they could provide to the leaders.

Simply setting up a mixed-race worker team — no matter how appropriate this decision — cannot reduce the sensitivity of the content discussed in a group like Ebony, or the feelings it evokes. Issues surrounding ethnicity, racism, and black, white or bicultural attempts to offer improved standards of care are painful and can easily put group members on the defensive. This was made worse in the Ebony foster carers' group by the suspicions group members brought with them. Being, by definition, all white, and alert to the prevailing criticisms of transracial placements, they suspected a hidden agenda amongst the group workers; that the latter were deliberately looking to find fault with their standards of child-rearing, perhaps even with a view to bringing their placements to a premature end. Such was the difficult context in which the leaders pursued their aims for the group by covering selected areas of content and by discussing and confronting members' reactions as these arose.

The matters briefly outlined above — of who the leaders and consultant were, the back-up they received from other agency staff, the natural defensiveness on the part of the group members, and the ways in which the workers tried to adhere to and use their ideas for group content despite this — will now be looked at, each in turn, in greater detail.

## *GROUP LEADERSHIP*

The Ebony foster carers' group was eventually run by three group workers, two black and one white. The issue of black only, or mixed leadership had been discussed at some length. The background to this debate was that the Ebony young people's groups had had, on each occasion, and for very good reasons, an all-black team of group workers. These group leaders had provided a positive role model and the opportunity for the group members to be in an all-black context, in some cases for the first time since babyhood. At first, this had caused the group members to feel very awkward and unsure of themselves in relating to black strangers. Initially members would not sit with or near the group leaders but took their chairs close to the walls of the fairly large room. Several had experience of being the only black child in otherwise all-white schools, as well as living in white families, so it is perhaps not surprising that they felt uncertain in such unfamiliar company. Ice-breaking and interaction games helped the group members and leaders to relax and relate to each other. Fairly quickly, the members began to feel safe enough to talk freely to the group workers, and soon they were enjoying the special freedom of being with others — both children and adults — who had had similar experiences to theirs and who therefore made it 'all right' to admit to what had happened and how they felt. The all-black leadership team also freed the workers to be confident of developing their own ideas about what was needed in the groups, based on their own black awareness and experience of growing up in a racist society.

For the foster carers' group, a mixed leadership seemed more appropriate, provided that it did not import the false notions of superiority/inferiority from wider society. To avoid this danger, it was determined that the 'lead' in each session and in each group exercise was to be taken either jointly or by one of the black workers. In the event, the two black and one white worker put a major effort into planning and running all the sessions on a joint basis. To have had only white leaders, whilst they would have shared experiences with the members and could have helped them to feel more at ease, would greatly have diluted the challenge to their thinking and assumptions which the group needed to provide. All black leaders, on the other hand, would have appeared very confrontational and would apparently have offered the members no one with whom to identify. Bicultural leaders seemed the ideal balance, provided that the black members of the leadership team were in the majority and hence did not appear to be an 'afterthought,' or tokenistic. It was considered particularly important to show the black workers in a strong and positive role so, through careful planning in sessions with their consultant, the group leaders ensured that activities in the group were built around this crucial factor.

## *GROUP CONSULTANT*

When it came to consultants, all the group workers in the project agreed that the sensitive nature of the group made it essential to hold feedback and planning sessions between group meetings with a consultant present, in order to run the group in the most effective way possible. Clearly, black consultants would have been preferable for both the young people's and the foster carers' groups, especially since the line managers in their agency were white. The shortage of black workers with time to spare and experience of the Ebony project at that time meant, however, that only one black consultant could be found, and the priority was for him to work with the all-black worker team from the young people's group. Consequently, the present author, a white person but someone with knowledge both about group work and about the Ebony project, became the consultant to the foster carers' group.

The author only agreed to take on this role knowing that the strenuous efforts to find a black consultant had failed. This difficulty in recruiting as consultants black individuals who had had enough experience both of child care practice and of group work was a fair reflection of the low level of recruitment of black staff in British social services departments at the time. This is slowly improving, particularly in those urban areas where there are large concentrations of black population. It is also a reflection of the comparatively low level of interest in group work in Britain, particularly in statutory agencies where it tends to be confined to a few, specialist areas of work such as the recruitment of foster parents and work with juvenile offenders. (It should be remembered that British social work courses train students generically; there is no separation of those studying group work, casework, etc.) Here, of course, the opportunity which projects like Ebony can provide for more workers to develop their group work skills are very valuable and have already meant that more black consultants will be available for Ebony in the future.

As consultant, the author's previous knowledge of the Ebony project and general experience in group work were useful, but she had to take care that she did not dilute the aims of the group or lessen its impact through unawareness of, or resistance towards a black perspective on her part. The author tried particularly hard, therefore, to develop a style which would facilitate the project's initiators and group workers to put their views most effectively into action. It was important that she gave space to the black group workers to express their concerns and what they felt was right in any given situation, as well as pointing them in new directions. Since the group's major concern was ethnicity, the reflections of the black workers on many aspects of its functioning were intrinsically more valid than her own. The consultant had to act as a facilitator and catalyst for them and, as far as possible, never as a block or a hindrance.

An ideal situation might well have been to have had a bicultural pairing of consultants working with the bicultural worker team. This would have allowed them freer rein to pick up on the subtle ways in which the group leaders related to one another and to the group members, particularly where ethnicity played a part in this. Since the other consultant could have acted as a safeguard against any unintentional racism on the author's own part, the author could perhaps have relaxed slightly more and given more attention to the detail of what the workers were feeding back. Also, in hindsight, and provided they had managed to establish the same kind of equal partnership as the group workers strove for, this could have been a useful way of introducing a less experienced black social worker to the role of consultant through working in tandem with the author.

## THE ROLE OF OTHER AGENCY STAFF

It is possible that group membership might have remained higher if the young people's social workers had continued throughout to stress the importance of the project to the foster carers. As it was, ambivalence about the value and purpose of the project on the part of these white social workers, and their lack of awareness of what was needed from them, presented difficulties throughout the project. This is a further instance of the way in which the relevance of ethnicity extends far beyond the group workers themselves – not only to their consultants and managers, but to the workers in the children's placing agency and beyond.

A further illustration of this was that culturally relevant material on each young person should have been provided by his or her social worker but was simply not available to the group workers. Comments such as "Winston is a West Indian mixed parentage child' are not specific enough either to help that young person to develop a positive image of himself, or to help his carers to provide him with detailed information about his cultural heritage. Many of the carers were embarrassed at not knowing exactly where in the West Indies their foster child's birth parents came from and, although they could have enquired more closely at the time of placement, it is fair to say that the agency had let them down badly in not routinely providing these details. Often, the social worker simply did not have enough background material available on any particular young person, never having realised the need for it before, and could not have provided a full social work assessment of his or her identity needs to accompany the referral. This is a reflection of the poor service which black clients are still tending to receive from predominantly white social work agencies in Britain. Little wonder, then, that there has been a tendency for black teams, black projects and black agencies to be set up to meet the needs of black service users, rather than continuing the pretense that predominantly white agencies, with ethnocentric policies, can offer an appropriately multicultural service.

In addition to the gaps in the background material they provided and the lukewarm way they supported their clients' group attendance, the follow-up work offered by the young people's social workers to their foster families after the group was, on the whole, insufficient. In order to assist the social workers with this task, one of the recommendations from the leaders and consultants was that, in the future, there should be regular opportunities to share with the young people's social workers the progress they and their carers were making in the groups. A formal mechanism would have helped this to happen and would also have ensured that the social workers did not neglect their responsibility for follow-up work.

## DEFENSIVENESS IN THE GROUP

Whereas the young people's groups were good fun to lead on both occasions, the foster carers' group was more difficult to plan. Whilst not wishing to blame the group members for the results of past departmental decisions (such as the making of transracial placements in the first place), the group leaders wanted to challenge members, as white people, to become better able to meet the racial and cultural needs of the black children they were caring for. It was important to strike a delicate balance between inspiring rethinking on the one hand, and driving group members into defensiveness on the other.

Where black children are already with white substitute carers, the question of what can and should be done to support these placements rises to the top of the agenda. With adoption placements, post-placement work is only just beginning to appear on the social work horizon in Britain and still, at the moment, carries connotations of the placement having 'failed' in some way if further professional input is needed. It is unlikely, therefore, that adoptive parents would be very ready to accept the kind of support which the Ebony project was offering. With foster families, on the other hand, there is the advantage of continuing agency involvement throughout the placement which provides the ideal context within which group work support can be offered.

It seems probable that the anxieties of the white foster carers who joined the Ebony group, and probably also of their individual social workers (since they too were white), were attributable to misapprehensions about the Ebony project. The myths surrounding this whole area of work in Britain can be strong enough to establish an all-pervasive atmosphere, yet sufficiently hidden to be extremely difficult to tackle in the group. It is important for the group workers to recognise these myths in order to be able to expose and challenge them. Underlying all the other myths may be a very general lay assumption about children — that their painful feelings should be left undisturbed because it is not good to see them upset. If any of the foster carers had not moved beyond this unhelpful view, then it is doubtful that they would have been able to work with the children on discussing information about their family and cultural backgrounds and heritage.

Secondly, transracial placements have become extremely controversial and policy and practice are moving sharply away from them. Although this is to be applauded, it may perhaps have left foster carers assuming that everything now considered bad about such placements is seen as their fault. Consequently, those carers who have existing transracial placements, and who offered their homes and their love at a time when these were gratefully enough received, are left to feel not only isolated and vulnerable, but also blamed, rejected and under attack. It was important to convince them in the group that the Ebony group workers saw them as having largely inherited the problems that agencies had bequeathed through their policies of earlier years. A further fear which the carers may have experienced was that the group would be used to gather adverse evidence about their transracial placements; even their referral to the group could have been seen as implied criticism of their abilities as carers. Ultimately, their greatest fear may have been that their foster child or children would be removed if the group leaders did not like what they heard in the group. It was important to establish right at the beginning that this was not the case and, in general, to bring these myths out into the open so as to provide reassurance.

Since the foster children were also attending a separate group in parallel with that attended by their foster parents, there were further areas of mythology which may have surrounded that group. Their foster parents may have suspected that the young people would all emerge from the group as militant black activists and, consequently, that they would no longer love, respect or want to live with their white foster families. The foster carers may have feared that the leaders of the young people's group all held extreme radical views, as opposed to balanced professional opinions that support such as that offered through the Ebony project was urgently needed. Even the fact of an all-black leadership team for the young people's group was probably a unique experience for the foster parents and, in itself, may have raised their anxiety levels about the project.

## *GROUP CONTENT*

Like recruitment, the content of the material used in the foster carers' group must be thought of in conjunction with that used in the young people's group because it was hoped that the carers and the young people would move through the same issues and stages of development in their respective groups roughly in parallel. It was felt that this would help them to continue the work at home between meetings and, also, that it would dispel some of the foster carers' fantasies about what their charges might be doing in their group. These fantasies were an unplanned factor in the groups. Both groups met at the same time, on the same night, in neighbouring rooms of the same building, to ease travel arrangements. The carers' anxieties that their quality of parenting was under scrutiny were raised in temperature every time there was any notable noise or silence next door. Even when the young people were having some particularly noisy fun, their carers wondered what they could be doing that they, the carers, were not able to share in. The original idea of having the two groups meeting over coffee part-way through the evening had to be abandoned after the first week because each carer dived straight onto his or her foster child and began pumping them for information. Any future parallel groups will probably be held in rooms at opposite ends of the building, or on different nights, so that the young people can be helped to feel free to share their experiences without regarding themselves as under the scrutiny of their carers or perhaps as being disloyal to them.

Group sessions of the foster parents' group used a variety of ways of presenting material. These ranged from a video on racial prejudice to brainstorming how the same underlying attitudes are reflected in the ways the words 'white' and 'black' are used in everyday language, and from a presentation on the geography and history of the Caribbean to a West Indian cookery evening culminating in a meal being eaten together by the two groups and their leaders. The members also shared their own experiences and those of their foster children at some length and, in the later stages of the group, discussed how changes in attitudes and better practice might be brought about by, for example, the use of libraries and other resource centers, mixing more with black people and learning about their lives, and exploring the facilities which the black community could offer, from black hairdressers to black churches. These topics all related closely to the group's aims as set out in an earlier section, and did reflect considerable progress made by group members as time went on.

Those who attended the carers' group were, in all but one case, at a very early stage, both in their straightforward knowledge about black issues and in their willingness to admit to the fact ours is a racist society and that we all share the responsibility for trying to change it for the better. Consequently, progress in the carers' group was slower than in the young people's group where the thirst for knowledge moved things along at a rapid pace. Nevertheless, the carers' group was important to its members as an opportunity to reflect on their previous complacency and to discuss their own and their foster children's needs for further information and greater awareness. A good example of this came in a session when many group members were busily denying the existence of widespread racial prejudice. To the extent that they did recognise it, they saw it as less of a problem for their foster children because they were protected in privileged white homes (Gill and Jackson, 1983). Eventually, one more aware person in the group explained what had happened to her foster daughter when she was singled out for unwarranted attention by the police. This 'freed' the group to be able to acknowledge further areas of discrimination, such as housing and employment — although they still felt that the young person's social worker should play the major role in tackling such problems, which consequently made them less of a concern to foster parents. Thus there was still some way to go before these carers would feel willing or able to assist their foster children in developing the emotional and social survival skills they will need as young black adults in Britain (Black and in Care Conference Report, 1985). The pre-determined length of eight weeks for the group (set because it ran in parallel with the young people's group) was really too short to allow this work to be pursued as far as it might have been.

In all sessions, the groupworkers gently persisted against rationalisation and denial. They accepted that opening up matters of identity, culture and discrimination with transracially placed foster children could well cause distress, but continued to advocate such honesty in the context of a warm and loving home. The price of avoiding painful issues now, could be a poorly adjusted or badly shaken young person later on, who would not be able to 'make it' in the harsh realities of the contemporary world. Questions of race will not go away and nor, therefore, will social workers' duty to provide a more effectively bicultural service. It was important to have a bicultural worker team conveying this message together. Race was not just the hobby-horse of the black workers, but a topic which all three demonstrated they considered to be crucial and unavoidable in its implications. The white worker was able to empathise with the pain and difficulty group members experienced in confronting issues such as their own racism, the impact of racial abuse and discrimination on their foster children, and their inability to offer any water-tight protection against this. The planning which the worker team undertook together ensured that, whilst she understood their feelings, the white worker did not rush in to protect group members from needing to pursue these issues to some workable conclusion, both within and beyond the group.

The helpful presence of one more aware group member in the carers' group, who also assisted the other members considerably in confronting painful issues, raises the question as to whether it would be effective in the future to plan for a more mixed membership, either in stages of awareness or, perhaps, in bringing together black and white foster parents in the same group. By the end of the group, the members were indeed expressing the opinion that it would have been helpful to have met some black foster carers, to have heard their views and experiences and learned from them. On the other hand, it was easier for them to say this with hindsight than it would have been to have felt safe enough to risk their views in mixed company in the very early stages of the group. Such an experience could also have been quite damaging for the black foster parents, both because the white carers were expressing some fairly overtly racist views early on, and because the responsibility for changing them might have seemed to descend too heavily onto the shoulders of the black foster parents.

## CONCLUSIONS

The foster parent's group was certainly not all plain sailing. It was difficult for the foster carers to build up sufficient trust to feel safe in re-examining their most entrenched attitudes. It seems certain too, that eight weeks is not a long enough period fully to overcome their fears, or to challenge deeply-held assumptions. It takes considerable time, for example, to demonstrate how the 'colour-blind' approach of treating all children exactly the same discriminates against black children because it neglects their particular needs, and still longer to begin to construct a new set of beliefs based on a greater awareness of the inevitable racism in our predominantly white society. Perhaps still more acknowledgement and praise for the love and care provided by the white carers, from all the workers involved in the group and outside it, might have helped to reduce the defensiveness which, to some extent, stayed throughout the group's life. Perhaps, also, within the overall fact that the Ebony project is designed to meet the children's needs, the group's aims could have focused more on the carers themselves and less on meeting the children's needs through them. The group could have started from identifying the foster parents' own perspective and negotiating aims with them; it might have been that, had they formulated an aim such as 'to help us provide the best possible experience for our foster child,' the group could have come round less defensively to seeing that this can only happen if members, too, are willing to change. The carers might then have felt more as if the social workers leading the groups were prepared to treat them as colleagues and more willing to change their views.

Nevertheless, the carers evaluated the group positively. They felt it had been a useful learning experience, and somewhere where they could meet others doing the same work as themselves, with whom to compare both the joys and the tribulations. They now felt less isolated. They also appreciated the valuable practical advice they had received and being alerted to useful resources such as the Commonwealth Institute in London, the destination of the very enjoyable joint outing at the end of the two groups. The foster carers who had attended the group now realised how little they knew about their foster children's birth families, and how important it was that they should have black friends. Finally, they recommended that all transracial foster parents should have the opportunity to join a group like the one to which they had belonged.

On both occasions when it has run, the Ebony project has amply proven its worth as an innovative and effective means of tackling a sensitive and badly neglected area of work. Amidst all the current attention being paid to same-race placements—vital though it is to support this as the only viable policy for the future (Small, 1986)—the needs of those carers and their foster children who are already living in stable, but often not well supported transracial placements can tend to be forgotten. Because the Ebony groups have shown one way in which this balance can begin to be redressed, the recommendations which stemmed from them stressed that they should no longer be organised on an ad hoc basis, but attendance should be an *expected* part of any transracial placement. This would achieve a degree of consistency in approach and would mean that Ebony's work was not marginalised. It would require the development, however, of adequate in-service training for potential group leaders and consultants, and continuing efforts to recruit more black professional staff.

The Ebony project also has wider implications. It represents only the tip of an iceberg in a sea of social work practice where so much has continued along time-worn lines and where agencies regularly fail to meet the challenging implications of the ethnicity of their clients. It has taken a predominantly black group of employees, like those involved in the Ebony project, to shake this complacency and to indicate better ways forward. The project has also shown the valuable role which group work can play in offering new alternatives. The young people's groups have been a glowing example of this. A number of withdrawn and confused young black people — lacking the range of positive black role models which the USA presents but not the negative media images of poverty, crime and general fecklessness amongst blacks which both our countries seem so ready to swallow — came together with strong black group workers for a celebration of their cultural heritage and an opportunity to take a fresh look at themselves and their own place in the world. Individual work simply cannot match the powerful new learning that occurs when members join together in groups. The group for foster carers was dealing with far more entrenched attitudes and was altogether a harder nut to crack, yet it probably provided a more typical example of the immense amount of challenging work which remains to be done before social services can really be offered sensitively to multi-ethnic communities. In helping the group's white members to rethink the implications of race and racism for themselves and their foster children, a bicultural worker team effectively modelled the combined efforts we must all make in moving practice on into the 1990's.

# REFERENCES

*Black and In Care Conference Report.* London: Children's Legal Centre, 1985.

Central Council for Education and Training in Social Work. *Requirements and Regulations for the Diploma in Social Work.* London:CCETSW, 1989, Paper 30.

Gil, O. and Jackson, B. *Adoption and Race: Black, Asian and Mixed race Children in White Families.* London: Batsford, 1983.

Loftus, Y. Black families and parental access. *Adoption and Fostering,* 1986, 10(4), 26-27.

Maxime, J.E. *Black Like Me.* London: Emani Publications, 1987.

Miller, D. Proud to be black. *Community Care,* 21st February 1985, 18-19.

Mullender, A. and Miller, D. The Ebony group: black children in white foster homes. *Adoption and Fostering,*1985, 9(1), 33-40 and 49.

Small, J. Transracial placements: conflicts and contradictions. In Ahmed, S., Cheetham, J. and Small, J. (Eds.), *Social work with black children and their families.* London: Batsford, 1986.

# Race, Color, Ethnicity, and Class: Issues of Biculturalism in School-Based Adolescent Counseling Groups

## David G. Bilides

**SUMMARY.** The issues of race, color, ethnicity, and class present many challenges for group workers leading adolescent counseling groups in culturally mixed urban areas. These issues are examined in detail in the context of a school-based group work program for middle school teenagers. The role of the group leader in working with this population is discussed, and guidelines are offered for developing biculturalism in group members and for addressing race, color, ethnicity, and class as they arise in bicultural group processes.

Group leaders who have survived adolescent counseling groups are fond of describing such groups as "challenging" to new group workers. When group members come from different cultural backgrounds, however, a challenging process can feel unworkable, even for an experienced group leader. This paper will discuss the issues of race, color, ethnicity, and class in a context of multicultural counseling groups for middle school adolescents. Its purpose is to

David G. Bilides, MSW, is affiliated with the Adolescent Therapeutic Day Schools, San Mateo County Mental Health Department, 225 W. 37th Avenue, San Mateo, CA 94403.

The author would like to thank the following people for their contributions, comments, suggestions, and support: Melanie Bruno, Amarilis Carrasquillo-Melendez, Dina Carbonell, Emily Carrington, Denise M. N. Daniel, Maggie Goodwin, Palmer Page, and Ceil Parteleno. Thanks also to Martha Yager, John Petersen, the Vinfen Corporation and Nancy Littlefield for technical assistance. Special thanks to Victoria Alexander and the Massachusetts Mental Health Center Scholars Program and School Consultation and Treatment Program for making this paper possible.

describe how these issues arise, how they affect group processes, and how group leaders can enhance the bicultural development of group members.

For the purposes of this discussion, the terms "race," "color," "ethnicity," and "class" are used to distinguish various ways in which group members identify and differentiate themselves. "Race" refers to an identification that the children make predominantly on the basis of skin color, other physical characteristics, and language. The adolescents at the school program under consideration assign four such subgroupings: Black, Spanish, White, and Asian. "Color" is specifically the color of a person's skin; "people of color" refers to all people except Whites. "Ethnicity," within a racial subgroup, is the family's geographical and cultural point of origin, as perceived by the individual. "Class" denotes the vertical stratification of individuals and families in society, based on economic resources. Finally, the term "bicultural" is both qualitative and dynamic. It refers not only to characteristics of individuals, groups, or situations involving more than one culture, but also to movement between different cultural contexts. The dynamics of the groups under consideration generate many, often simultaneous bicultural processes, resulting in "multicultural" groups.

A review of the literature in the preparation of this article found little relevant to bicultural dynamics in children's groups. Bicultural processes referred most frequently to Black-White interactions of adults in individual treatment. Color was seldom mentioned, usually in the context of a light-to-dark hierarchy. There was a wide range of opinions on the importance of ethnicity, and class, when dealt with at all, was seen as a powerful variable. The interested reader is directed to the bibliography for further exploration.

## THE BRACETTI GROUP WORK PROGRAM

The Mariana Bracetti Middle School (a pseudonym) is located in Boston and serves a population of 700 adolescents in grades six through eight. The students, aged 11 to 16, come from a variety of cultural backgrounds. Fifty-five percent are Latino (predominantly Puerto Rican), forty percent are Black (primarily Afro-American with a sizeable Caribbean minority), and the rest are a mix of mostly White (Irish and Greek) and Asian (mostly Cambodian and Laotian). The vast majority of students come from inner-city, low income families.

The Bracetti Human Services Collaborative is staffed by social workers from two agencies within walking distance of the school. The four full-time Black, Latino, and White clinicians and their part-time co-workers have office and counseling space in the school. The primary goal of the Bracetti Collaborative is to address student problems that arise from a variety of psychosocial causes or cultural differences at the earliest possible point of intervention. The social services offered seek to avert the cycle of low achievement, low skills attainment, and concomitant problems, such as early school dropout, poor survival skills, teenage pregnancy, and unemployment. The Collaborative offers individual, family, and group counseling, as well as crises intervention and consultation services.

The overall goal of the Collaborative's group counseling program is to help students develop decision-making skills, combat social isolation, clarify values and cultural differences, and promote constructive group behavior and intercultural contact and interaction. Students are referred to the program by teachers, administrators, or parents, but the most fruitful source of referrals is the students themselves. Prospective group members are screened through individual interviews and classroom observations. Groups, run in English and Spanish, meet weekly for 10 to 20 sessions throughout the school year. Issues of race, color, ethnicity, and class arise often in these groups, and their influences on group processes are described in the following sections.

## RACE

There are many ways in which race affects group process in the Collaborative groups. It is probably the primary determinant of roles taken by subgroups. These subgroup roles reflect sociocultural patterns, mirror the power structure of the school, and usually inhibit bicultural fluidity of the members in the early stages of group development. In general, the groups become microcosms of struggles and prejudices played out in larger social contexts. The most obvious example of this dynamic is in seating arrangements. In the initial sessions of the group the members subgroup by race in their choice of seats, even if they know each other from school classes or in their neighborhood.

Group attendance is another indicator of the effects of race. A student will usually drop out of a group if he or she is the only representative of a racial group among the members. Students need a built-in support system, whether a subgroup or other similar children or an alliance with a group leader of the same race. This is especially true if the racial group to which a student belongs has little power in the school.

One recurring theme in the Bracetti groups is cultural typecasting of Blacks as aggressive troublemakers and of Latinos as subdued, obedient, hard-working students. This contrasts with the lack of general typecasting of the White or Asian students. The Asians are quite new to the school and are different enough that no one knows quite what to make of them. Sometimes, however, other students typecast them on the basis of martial arts movies — their most familiar context.

Group issues are frequently framed in terms of race. Membership definition or exclusion becomes racially based when outsiders are involved, e.g., on field trips. Power struggles commonly begin with racial motifs. On the other hand, it is often in racial relationship to the leader that members begin breaking anti-bicultural patterns, either by uniting against the leader, or through experiencing emotional conflict between personal feelings and long-held stereotypes.

## COLOR

The color hierarchy (light experienced as superior to dark) is analogous to racial subgrouping in that initially it obstructs biculturalism. Paradoxically, it can also link culturally different members who bond on the basis of their color status.

Comments about skin color and other physical characteristics come up frequently in these multicultural groups. Clear examples are those in which color is specifically mentioned in a member's

comment—"Just 'cause you're light you think you're so good"—
or where a physical characteristic becomes a topic of discussion: "I
don't want no nappy hair."

The color hierarchy also arises in less overt ways.

> In one girls' group the members were asked to make a col-
> lage showing how they would like to see themselves if they
> were high fashion models. Through the collages, the Latina
> girls wanted to be lighter-skinned even though they were light,
> and the Black girls wanted to be lighter and have long, straight
> hair. The group leader (who was Black) deliberately cut out a
> picture of a black-skinned woman with a short Afro. The girls
> asked, "What's so nice about having short, kinky hair?"
> When the leader pointed out that the collages were not reflec-
> tive of the girls, that they all wanted lighter skin, and asked
> why they thought that was, they answered, "Look at TV, look
> at models. If you look like that, everyone will like you." (In-
> terestingly, the one dissenting view was held by the darkest-
> skinned girl in the group, who was from Nigeria. She said, "I
> can't understand why people want to be light-skinned.")
> In a boys' group run by a Black male, members were asked
> to look at several pictures of Black women and choose the one
> they thought was the most beautiful. The boys chose the
> lighter-skinned women. When the boys were asked why they
> thought the women were beautiful, they said they didn't know.

The latter group leader has observed that the darker-skinned children in his groups are either pushed to the side or they overcompen-
sate and are very vocal and energetic. He makes an analogy with
gangs in which the darker-skinned children are the leaders. The
peer group becomes the place where they can gain power, but it is a
negative kind of power—often the only type that young, Black
males have. This dynamic is not limited to boys, however. In a
girls' group run by White co-leaders, the two darkest-skinned girls
were the ones who challenged the leaders the most and who raised
Black/White concerns.

## ETHNICITY

To begin with, students are usually not sure what "ethnicity" means. It takes a short discussion, questions about their parents, and real-life examples on the group leader's part to connect the word to the members' personal understanding of the topic. Students are already adept at naming and exploiting ethnic divisions; the impact on biculturalism is predictable.

The Black racial group breaks down into ethnic subgroups: Blacks born in the United States ("American," or "we Blacks") and those born in the Caribbean Islands and Africa ("foreign Blacks"). Foreign-born Blacks have assimilation problems within the Black racial group and are seen as uncouth, pushy or simply weird. The ethnic scapegoats in previous years were the Jamaicans, due to their accent, perceived aggressiveness, supposed overinvolvement in drugs and crime, and dark skin color. Over the past year, Haitians have become the new scapegoats, also on account of their accent and skin color, but additionally due to rumors about AIDS, jokes about "boat people," and unfamiliar customs.

Even American Blacks subdivide, at times, into Northern and Southern Blacks. In one group, a girl raised in the South was finding it difficult to adjust to northern Black culture. She told the group she missed the safety of the South. Northern children sometimes make fun of the slower manner and speech of many Southern Blacks.

The Latino racial group in the Northeast breaks down most often into Puerto Rican and Dominican ethnic factions. Each group tends to look down on the other and has various derogatory names they call each other. The Dominicans see themselves as "real Hispanics," superior to the Puerto Ricans, yet are also envious of them for their legal status as U.S. citizens. Dominicans will sometimes "pass" as Puerto Ricans for legal reasons or to obtain employment, or they will stay over in Puerto Rico, hoping to go to the United States. The Puerto Ricans resent this.

There are other immigration-related tensions. For example, the Dominicans are more recent immigrants to Boston. The older immigrants' children tend to be more self-assured and confrontive in their relationships with adult authority figures, and in that way were described by one Uruguayan group leader as being perceived as more like Black children (i.e., more "Americanized") by her Latino group members.

Language is a major sub-issue of ethnicity. For Latino children, speaking Spanish is not just an expression of identity but is used in groups to form alliances with some members, exclude others, or communicate covertly. Spanish-speaking members will also use English in the group to distance what they are saying from family, community, or cultural norms. This happens especially with expressions of disrespect (e.g., swearing), statements which do not involve feelings, and discussion of illicit topics such as drugs.

## *CLASS*

Class issues are often intertwined with those of race, color, and ethnicity. Since being White or light-skinned is seen as a status symbol, among Latinos, "marrying lighter" is encouraged to raise the social status of individuals and their families. Upper classes strive to maintain what one Puerto Rican group leader calls "beigeness." As an example of the interaction between the issues of class and color she cites the two large waves of Cuban migration. The first, after the revolution, were lighter-skinned upper classes and denied their blackness. The second wave, the Marielitos, contained more Blacks and more lower class Cubans. For Central Americans class is played out not only through skin color but also by the extent to which one has recognizable native ("Indian") features.

Whereas the Bracetti children are diverse in terms of race, ethnicity, and color, most are from low income families. Thus, class issues usually unify the group against the outside society (i.e., those with higher incomes). The poorest group members (e.g., those living in shelters) are sometimes teased about their clothing, and everyone disparages those who are on "welfare." One group leader believes that students' class status is the most difficult topic for them to deal with in group sessions. A group that will talk readily about racial problems will avoid discussing poverty.

More often than not, intragroup class struggles occur when recent immigrants experience a lowering of class prestige but not of class attitudes or values.

In one group of Spanish-speaking children a middle class girl from Guatemala began to lecture the other members about their "bad behavior" and referred to her life back in Guatemala. The other children resented her preachy style and responded angrily with comments such as, "But you're here, what's wrong with it [here]?"

## THE ROLE OF THE GROUP LEADER

A number of articles offer suggestions to people working with what are still called "minority" populations. It seems generally assumed that most counselors are White and that they work with individuals rather than groups. Some authors discuss stereotypes (e.g., Smith, 1977), or talk about what is different about working with a specific racial or cultural group (e.g., Ruiz and Padilla, 1977; Markward, 1979; and Brown, 1984).

Other authors present broader models for counseling with culturally different populations. Devore and Schlesinger (1981) describe a model of social work practice that is sensitive to issues of ethnicity and class. They believe that counselors need to develop layers of bicultural awareness and understanding. The model (elaborated by Steiner and Devore, 1983) emphasizes group as well as individual history, including experiences of oppression and migration, as well as beliefs and customs; a focus on the present; a thorough grounding in the client's "ethnic reality" (which includes class); and an understanding that unconscious phenomena can affect functioning.

Sue's model (1977) anticipates this process and speaks directly to the culture- and class-bound values and language factors inherent in White counseling theories. Sue iterates the need for knowledge of "minority" group cultures and experiences, checking of value assumptions, an ongoing process to monitor the counseling, and goals that meet the client's needs.

McNeely and Badumi (1984) suggest that bicultural encounters are also affected by race-linked conversational differences. They describe six patterns of verbal and non-verbal communication that require the counselor's attention.

Lum (1982) and Pinderhughes (1984) highlight the political dimensions of bicultural counseling. Pinderhughes, for example, elevates ethnicity (synonymous with cultural identity) to the highest significance in the clinical encounter and links it to the dynamics of power and powerlessness that occur in any treatment relationship. She believes that the clinician's understanding of her or his own cultural identity is of critical importance, especially for White and middle class workers. Pinderhughes also has developed an experiential training group to help clinicians become more sensitive to cultural differences, stereotyping, and bias. The training involves raising bicultural awareness through personal examinations of ethnic background, ethnic values, race, color, class, and power.

## PUTTING UNDERSTANDING INTO PRACTICE

Once group leaders have attained new levels of bicultural awareness, how can that understanding be put into practice with groups? This section provided guidelines and case examples to help group leaders use their knowledge in addressing issues of race, color, ethnicity, and class as a way of facilitating group process and enhancing the bicultural development of group members.

1. Confront the issue.

In one career exploration group the members had divided themselves along a narrow table into two subgroups: the Spanish-speaking students at one end, and the Black students at the other. The members of each subgroup were conversing among themselves, the Spanish-speaking children using Spanish. The group leader interrupted and said, "It looks as though we have two groups: the Black kids here, and the Spanish-speaking kids here. What do you make of that?" The students at first protested that it wasn't a matter of two different groups. The group leader persisted by asking them to explain the seating arrangement. A discussion ensued about "being with people you know" and how people get to know other people. The members spontaneously changed their seats to create a more mixed arrangement.

Confrontation is especially necessary when the group dynamics threaten to replicate the day-to-day oppression experienced by the children. When issues of race, color, ethnicity, and class are discussed openly, the group becomes safer and a place where bicultural interaction and learning can occur more easily.

2. Go back to the group rules. Most groups have rules about respecting other members, no name calling ("capping"), no put downs, and so on. When members use racial or ethnic slurs, one method for handling the situation is first to deal with it, as one would deal with any other verbal insult. It is important, however, to go on and explore the nature of the particular insult.

> A Black group member told another member, "Get away from me you Puerto Rican bitch." After dealing with the "bitch" part of the insult, the group leader asked the member, "What does her being Puerto Rican have to do with how angry you are at her?" The group then discussed how and why people use racial and ethnic terms to insult others.

Such exploration begins to break down the walls created by racial subgroup isolationism and ethnic divisiveness, thereby enhancing biculturalism.

3. Discuss stereotypes at all levels: personal, familial, and societal. One way of doing this is to point out how specific comments can become generalizations about an entire population.

> One group of six Puerto Rican girls were discussing the members' experiences with Dominican boyfriends. They believed that Dominican men had a strong sense of machismo and had to have several women; Puerto Rican men were more easygoing. The group leaders asked several question: "Why might this be true?" "Is it true of all Dominican and Puerto Rican men?" "What do other people say about Puerto Ricans and Dominicans in general?" The group discussed how such generalizations can be harmful.

Another way to handle stereotypes is to discuss how children learn them. It is useful to move from family and peers to societal means of indoctrination, such as media images.

In the group described earlier in which boys were asked to pick the most beautiful women from a set of pictures, the group members, unable at first to articulate why they made the choices they did, finally acknowledged the preponderance of light-skinned women in their selections. They discussed where people might learn that light skin was more beautiful than dark skin (e.g., from watching television) and why people might think that.

4. Point out commonalities. Although group members may come from different countries, cultures, and neighborhoods, they are alike in many ways by virtue of being adolescents and dealing with the issues of that life stage. When these linkages are explored, bi-cultural pathways are opened up.

One girls' group was discussing favorite places to go to hear music. The White girls talked about going to White clubs to hear punk music, the Puerto Rican girls described Puerto Rican clubs and salsa, and the Black girls mentioned rapping in Black clubs. The girls could identify with each other's pleasure in going out and listening to music. The group leader than asked them about parties. All the girls agreed that parties were not safe for them, that the underlying rule was, "Be out by eight." After eight the hoods usually showed up with their weapons. Since, in reality, none of the girls went to clubs very much, this discussion moved into another common theme: there's nothing safe for teens to do.

Another group composed of two White, two Puerto Rican, two Afro-American, and two Haitian girls, began to discuss how others made fun of them. One White girl mentioned that she was teased for being White. Then a Haitian girl said that she was made fun of for wearing her hair a certain way. A Puerto Rican girl followed by saying she was called "Hurricane Inez" because she was seen as hysterical, and that all Spanish-speaking girls were perceived as overemotional. The discussion continued, with the group leader underlining the commonalities and at the same time implicitly giving the members permission to talk about being different.

Another commonality children of color in the groups share is the necessity and difficulty of being bicultural, of grappling with two sets of values: their own culture's and those of a dominant White society with which they must come to terms. Since similar problems arising from this conflict are experienced by children of color, an open discussion can facilitate their mutual bicultural development.

5. Explore the meaning of words and language.

The members of a boys' group started insulting one boy by saying that he was on welfare. The group leader, after ascertaining from the group that this was meant as an insult and dealing with that, asked the boys how they would know someone was on welfare and what "being on welfare" means. The leader was able to use the boys' vague answers to move the discussion from a questionable assumption on one member's financial status to a group acknowledgement of common class status in the larger society and the meaning for them of that status.

In another boy's group the members were asked to stage a role play of their choosing. A drug-dealers-versus-the-cops scene was played out, during which one Spanish-speaking boy said to a Black boy, "Get against that wall, nigger, you ugly Black." During a subsequent discussion of the role play the group leader asked, "Why does he have to be ugly? Is he ugly?" "No." "Well, why did you say that, then?" "I hear people say that." "So, you're saying something someone else said, not what you feel." The leader pointed out how children from different cultures not only use racial and ethnic slurs, but sometimes don't even know what they're saying. They just know it's an insult.

As was mentioned earlier, bilingual Hispanic children often use English and Spanish selectively. The group leader needs to be sensitive to language shifts and choices, as they might relate to the content of the group session, and to stated language preferences apart from fluency. In the following example, this issue was the focus of an unsuccessful attempt at enhancing biculturalism.

One bilingual boy whose English skills were better than his Spanish skills refused to continue in an English monolingual group. He joined the analogous Spanish monolingual group, stating that he didn't feel comfortable in the other group, that they didn't like Hispanics. He felt powerless in the first group and expressed a fairly common attitude: "They don't let us talk; they talk all of the time."

In some of the Spanish monolingual groups the members speak Spanglish, or Spanish with many English words thrown in. This can be a problem for members who speak only Spanish. One Puerto Rican group leader deals with this by pretending she doesn't speak English even though the children know she does.

6. Recognize and acknowledge your own discomfort about race, color, ethnicity, and class issues.

In one group of two Black, two White, and three Latina girls the White group leader was asked by one of the Black girls why she wore black clothes so often. The leader's assertion that she liked black clothes did not prevent the question being raised weekly by group members. In supervision the worker initially expressed feeling uncomfortable with the focus on her clothes, but soon admitted that the underlying issue was that she felt uncomfortable and guilty about being White with this group of girls. Furthermore, there had been cross-racial tensions among the group members. The worker was encouraged to wear as much black as possible to the next session and to lead the inevitable to physical and other differences among the group members, including race, color, and ethnicity. Over the next several sessions the focus on the leader's wardrobe diminished, and cross-racial tensions became personalized and were discussed openly.

The group leader's role is extraordinarily difficult in these types of groups. The issues raised can stir up emotions intimately tied to the worker's identity. There are many traps to fall into; for example, emotional identification with one subgroup may lead to overcompensation for another, or differences of "style" between culturally different co-leaders may actually be the acting out of stereotyped roles or perceptions.

## CONCLUSION

Adolescents need sensitive and self-aware group leaders who can relate in a warm and genuine way. The leader can be a sounding board, an information giver, and educator, a mediator, a safety net, or a role model. Children also can learn about themselves and others from a group leader who is different from them. The main challenge is to create an environment that is safe and accepting enough to allow children of different races, colors, ethnicities, and classes to interact in new and positive ways. Ultimately they can acquire enough confidence and understanding to be capable of moving freely between different cultures. With sufficient preparation, a love and concern for children, cultural awareness and sensitivity, and a good sense of humor, this creation becomes exhilaratingly possible.

## REFERENCES

Amir, Y., "Contact hypothesis in ethnic relations," *Psychological Bulletin*, Vol. 71, No. 5 (May 1969), pp. 319-342.

Bilides, D., "Reaching inner-city children: a group work program model for a public middle school," *Proceedings of the 9th Symposium of the International Association for the Advancement of Social Work with Groups*, publication forthcoming.

Brayboy, T., "Black and white groups and therapists," in Milman, D., and Goldman, G., eds., *Group Process Today: Evaluation and Perspective*, Springfield, IL, Charles C Thomas, 1974, pp. 177-183.

Brayboy, T., "The black patient in group therapy," *International Journal of Group Psychotherapy*, Vol. 21, No. 3 (July 1971), pp. 288-293.

Brown, J., "Group work with low-income Black youth," *Social Work with Groups*, Vol. 7, No. 3 (Fall 1984), pp. 111-124.

Clore, G. et al., "Interracial attitudes and behavior at a summer camp," *Journal of Personality and Social Psychology*, Vol. 36, No. 2 (February 1978), pp. 107-116.

Cobbs, P., "Ethnotherapy in groups," in Solomon, L., and Berzon, B., eds., *New Perspectives on Encounter Groups*, San Francisco, Jossey-Bass, 1972, pp. 383-403.

Davis, L., "Essential components of group work with Black Americans," *Social Work with Groups*, Vol. 7, No. 3 (Fall 1984), pp. 97-109.

Davis, L., "Racial balance—a psychological issue: a note to group workers," *Social Work with Groups*, Vol. 3, No. 2 (Summer 1980), pp. 75-86.

Davis, L., "Racial composition of groups," *Social Work*, Vol. 24, No. 3 (May-June 1974), pp. 208-213.

Delgado, M., and Humm-Delgado, D., "Hispanics and group work: a review of the literature," *Social Work with Groups*, Vol. 7, No. 3 (Fall 1984), pp. 85-96.

Devore, W., and Schlesinger, E. *Ethnic-sensitive Social Work Practice*. St. Louis: C. V. Mosby. 1981.

Gergen, K., "The significance of skin color in human relations," in Franklin, J., *Color and Race*, Boston, Houghton-Mifflin, 1968, pp. 112-128.

Gibbs, J., "City girls: psychological adjustment of urban black adolescent females," *Sage: Scholarly Journal of Black Women*, Vol. 2, No. 2 (Fall 1985), pp. 28-36.

Gibbs, J., "Identity and marginality: issues in the treatment of biracial adolescents," *American Journal of Orthopsychiatry*, Vol. 57, No. 2 (April 1987), pp. 265-278.

Hardy-Fanta, C., and Montana, P., "The Hispanic female adolescent: a group therapy model," *International Journal of Group Psychotherapy*, Vol. 32, No. 3 (July 1982), pp. 351-366.

Hardy-Fanta, C., "Social action in Hispanic groups," *Social Work*, Vol. 31, No. 2 (March-April 1986), pp. 119-123.

Jacobson, C., "Separatism, integrationism and avoidance among black, white, and Latin adolescents," *Social Forces*, Vol. 55, No. 4 (June 1977), pp. 1011-1027.

Katlin, F., "The impact of ethnicity," *Social Casework*, Vol. 63, No. 3 (March 1982), pp. 168-171.

Lum, D., "Toward a framework for social work practice with minorities," *Social Work*, Vol. 27, No. 3 (May-June 1982), pp. 244-249.

Markward, M., "Group process and Black adolescent identity crisis," *School Social Work Journal*, Vol. 3, No. 2 (1979), pp. 78-84.

Matthews, J. *The Effect of Client's Race/Ethnic Status and Level of Acculturation, and the Influence of Practitioners' Characteristics on Social Workers' Clinical Judgements*. DSW. New York: Columbia University. May 1987.

McNeely, R., and Badumi, N., "Interracial communication in school social work," *Social Work*, Vol. 29, No. 1 (January-February 1984), pp. 22-26.

Pinderhughes, E., "Teaching empathy: ethnicity, race and power at the cross-cultural treatment interface," *The American Journal of Social Psychiatry*, Vol. 4, No. 1 (Winter 1984), pp. 5-12.

Prunty, H. et al., "Confronting racism in inner-city schools," *Social Work*, Vol. 22, No. 3 (1977), pp. 10-13.

Ransford, H., "Skin color, life chances, and anti-white attitudes," *Social Problems*, Vol. 18, No. 2 (Fall 1970), pp. 164-179.

Ruiz, R., and Padilla, A., "Counseling Latinos," *Personnel and Guidance Journal*, Vol. 55, No. 7 (March 1977), pp. 410-428.

Sebring, D., "Considerations in counseling interracial children," *Journal of Non-White Concerns in Personnel and Guidance*, Vol. 13, No. 1 (January 1985), pp. 3-9.

Sladen, B., "Effects of race and socioeconomic status on the perception of process variables in counseling," *Journal of Counseling Psychology*, Vol. 29, No. 6 (November 1982), pp. 560-566.

Smith, E., "Counseling Black individuals: some stereotypes," *Personnel and Guidance Journal*, Vol. 55, No. 7 (March 1977), pp. 390-396.

Steiner, J., and Devore, W., "Increasing descriptive and prescriptive theoretical skills to promote ethnic-sensitive practice," *Journal of Education for Social Work*, Vol. 19, No.2 (Spring 1983), pp. 63-70.

Sue, D., "Counseling the culturally different: a conceptual analysis," *Personnel and Guidance Journal*, Vol. 55, No. 7 (March 1977), pp. 422-426.

Teplin,L., "A comparison of racial ethnic preferences among Anglo, Black, and Latino children," *American Journal of Orthopsychiatry*, Vol. 46, No. 4 (October 1976), pp. 702-709.

Udry, J. et al., "Skin color, status, and mate selection," *American Journal of Sociology*, Vol. 76, No. 4 (January 1971), pp. 722-733.

Wong, W. *Impact of Ethnic Status on Social Work Clinical Judgements*. Ph.D. Denver, CO. August 1982.

# The Ethnic Group Experience

## Donna E. Hurdle

**SUMMARY.** Multi-ethnic therapeutic groups are an increasingly common form of intervention in human service settings. Cultural diversity affects the group dynamics in predictable ways. Three dynamics are discussed in the paper: recapitulation of the family of origin, group culture and group as a microcosm of society. Transcultural group intervention enables members to discuss culturally influenced behavior patterns, value systems and communication styles. Leaders facilitate the acquisition of improved multi-cultural relationship skills and an enriched ethnic consciousness. Members are encouraged to teach each other about their cultural heritage and in so doing improve their bicultural adaptation skills. Multi-ethnic groups become a laboratory for learning about cultural differences and human similarities, as well as a forum to address personal life issues.

## INTRODUCTION

Theoretical development of practice theories in recent years has moved toward a generic perspective. There is a significant absence of principles concerning practice geared toward persons of color (Lum, 1982). While social workers have traditionally recognized the special needs of minority clients, the lack of specialized practice theory may result from current emphases on other priorities, such as systems theory and effectiveness, as well as the lack of a unified methodology for minority practice (Lum).

However, despite this overall trend, several authors have articulated an ethnic-sensitive approach to practice. Devore and Schle-

Donna E. Hurdle, MSW, ACSW, is a doctoral candidate, College of Social Work, University of South Carolina. Her current position is Director of Program Development, Association for Retarded Citizens, Anchorage, AK.

singer (1987) encourage practitioners to use a dual perspective — an awareness that ethnic clients live in two worlds, that of the dominant culture as well as that of a unique cultural community with separate values, traditions, language, family structures, etc. This theme originated with Norton (1978) who referred to the dominant culture as the sustaining environment of institutional systems and the ethnic community as the nurturing environment.

Granger and Portner (1985) identify the bias of educational institutions in teaching Anglo-Euro-American principles and values as if they apply to all humans in all places. Social work practitioners, while aware of discrimination and oppression against people of color, often fail to value the unique adaptive differences and sense of ethnic identify of minority persons.

Frequently, the literature on therapeutic intervention with minority clients emphasizes methodology directed toward combatting oppression and discrimination (Granger & Portner, 1985; Hopps, 1982). Other practice strategies suggest using indigenous treatment methods and other culturally based methods of resolving conflict, both interpersonal and intrapersonal (Ito, 1985; Manson, Walker & Kivahan, 1987). The use of natural support systems is also frequently recommended (Granger & Portner, 1985; Delgado & Humm-Delgado, 1982). While these suggestions may be of great value in individual or family intervention, they offer limited guidance for social workers who lead therapeutic groups composed of members from culturally and ethnically diverse backgrounds.

Therapeutic groups are widely used in mental health and other human service settings in the United States. Many groups are multi-ethnic in composition due to the diverse cultural populations of American cities. Clinical practitioners are in need of theoretical and practice methodologies for multi-ethnic group work. The purpose of this paper is to discuss the dynamics operating in multi-ethnic groups and to offer culturally appropriate intervention responses. Skillful transcultural therapeutic treatment of multi-ethnic groups can enhance the cultural identity of ethnic members and facilitate the development of bicultural skills. Group members learn to develop positive multi-cultural relationships through interaction with persons from diverse ethnic backgrounds and to recognize their internalized bias and prejudice. The group experience, therefore, offers a vehicle for personal problem-solving as well as exploration of cross-cultural issues.

## MULTI-ETHNIC GROUP WORK

Therapeutic groups are a frequently used method of service delivery in various mental health settings. They are cost effective, serving multiple clients per treatment hour, and have proved to be of significant therapeutic value (Yalom, 1985). The experience of ethnic clients in groups has received limited theoretical attention. Frequently there is a focus on a specific ethnic group, and often on a particular type of problem (Edwards & Edwards, 1984; Lee, Juan & Hom, 1984; Ashby, Gilchrist & Miramontez, 1987; Goldberg, Kestenbaum & Shebar, 1987). The literature on therapy with specific ethnic groups will be of limited value to the practitioner in understanding the dynamic interplay of persons from diverse cultural backgrounds. While therapists would profit from an understanding of the unique culture of various ethnic members, an integrated and holistic perspective is also needed. Multi-ethnic therapy groups will have different dynamics and issues than homogenous groups (Tsui & Schultz, 1988).

Chau (1989) offers concept of socio-cultural dissonance as an organizing principle for a conceptual formulation of group work practice with ethnic minority populations. He identifies four areas of concern that can be addressed through group work intervention: ethnic adaptation, interethnic integration, ethnic consciousness raising and ethnic rights. Ethnic minority clients will frequently bring these concerns into a multi-ethnic therapeutic group. Chau delineates different goals and intervention strategies for each locus of concern. Strategies such as socialization training, value clarification, cultural awareness and empowerment are very appropriate for therapeutic groups.

There are a multitude of complex interpersonal dynamics that operate in multi-ethnic groups. Ethnic minority group members have a particular set of issues and concerns, as discussed by Chau (1989). Majority group members also have unique issues. In addition, all members will have personal reactions to race and ethnicity, including varying levels of bias and prejudice.

Multi-ethnic groups are an opportunity for members to address their reactions to cultural diversity, as well as to develop problem-solving skills to handle their individual life concerns. It is imperative that clinicians identify the unique dynamics of multi-ethnic groups in order to develop appropriate interventions.

Using the theoretical base of Yalom's (1985) principles of group psychotherapy, three significant dynamics will be described in this paper. Yalom's theory has been chosen due to its wide acceptance as an empirically valid methodology and its use as a foundation theoretical model in many graduate social work programs. Each dynamic will be discussed with case illustrations; suggestions will be made to enable therapists to develop a positive multi-cultural group experience.

## RECAPITULATION OF FAMILY OF ORIGIN

Therapeutic group members interact with leaders and other members as they may once have interacted with their family of origin. This transference phenomena is also seen in individual therapeutic methods, but is perhaps more powerful in group due to the presence of multiple members, leading to issues of competition for attention from the leader(s). Yalom (1985) refers to this dynamic of replication of family interaction as "recapitulation of the primary family group," and suggests that individual clients may behave in a variety of ways, such as becoming very dependent upon the leaders or defying them, competing with other members for leader attention or attempting to split or create rivalry between co-therapists. These patterns are based on a nuclear family experience.

Many ethnic clients, however, grow up in an extended family network quite dissimilar to the nuclear family. Native American tribal groups, for example, often parent communally. Children live with aunts and uncles as frequently as with biological parents. Lines of kinship are often loosely defined, with all members of the tribal group referred to as kin. The psychological parents of these children may be more appropriately seen as the kinship network rather than the biological parents. Filipino communal families are quite similar, as are aboriginal people in many parts of the world. Other ethnic groups, such as the Amish, Hasidic Jews and Italians, while valuing the role of biological parents, strongly involve the extended family and larger ethnic community in the rearing of children.

When ethnic persons participate in a group experience, their relationships with the leader and other group members will be based on their unique family of origin experience. Native Americans may experience the group, once trust and rapport are developed, as an extended family and feel quite comfortable in sharing personal concerns and participating in giving feedback to others. However, Asian-Americans may view the group of multiple strangers as a threat. Lee, Juan and Hom (1984) suggest that group leaders should seek approval from the formal or informal family leader for the participation of a family member in group. If the family member then becomes a member of the group, they will experience the leader as "part of the family" and rank order the other members as naturally occurs in Asian families. From these examples, it is clear that very different group experiences will result for ethnic persons as compared to Caucasian clients. This leads to questions about the appropriateness of homogenous versus heterogenous groups, and the ethnicity of the group leader in comparison to group members.

It is imperative that group leaders have an understanding of the ethnic background of group members in order to correctly interpret client behavior. Explicit discussion of ethnic background, family of origin dynamics and the connection to present group experience may be a method of addressing this concern.

This dynamic of recapitulation of the ethnic family was illustrated by a situation occurring in a group for mothers of incest victims. A Filipino client's pre-teen daughter had been molested by her second husband, the child's step-father. Group leaders became concerned that the client displayed little empathy for her daughter and excused her husband's behavior while maintaining frequent contact with him as he lived outside the home by court order. The client demonstrated a lack of affect about the molest situation, stating she had resolved her feelings shortly after the disclosure.

After consultation with the author, the group leaders began to explore cultural factors impacting the client's behavior. The client gradually revealed her understanding that incest was a common experience in the Filipino culture; one that she herself had experienced in her youth. The client was aware of a number of women in her extended family who had also endured these incidents, and was unaware of any legal or social sanctions against this behavior.

Upon learning of these cultural family patterns, the leaders were able to understand the client's behavior within the context of her ethnic heritage. This led to a re-evaluation of their assessment of the client's methods of coping and a re-interpretation of her emotional responses. The therapeutic focus in this client's case was quite different than that with clients raised in the United States where a strong prohibition against incest exists.

## GROUP CULTURE

All therapeutic groups develop a culture based on norms and types of interactions existing in the group. The group leader plays a large role in the creation of the group culture by his/her comments, expectations and encouragement or discouragement of behaviors. most group leaders have been trained in a method requiring verbalization of thoughts and feelings and confrontation of conflict, paralleling the cultural values of Caucasian America. Ethnic clients are frequently confused and anxious when faced with these expectations. Asian clients may find these requirements antithetical to traditional values where personal matters are never revealed to outsiders (Tsui & Schultz, 1988). Native Americans develop relationships through silence and it is important to avoid asking personal relationships early in a professional relationship (Edwards & Edwards, 1984). These examples indicate that a group leader's training in asking questions to probe feelings may be highly inappropriate for various ethnic clients. This may seriously impair trust development and result in client drop out or resistance.

An illustration of this dynamic occurred in a group for dependent women operating in a community mental health center. A Native American woman's behavior was quite different from the verbal interaction of Caucasian clients, who composed the other members of the group. The Native American client was very quiet, rarely initiated conversation and frequently failed to maintain eye contact. Group leaders, also Caucasian, began to label the client's behavior as resistant or resulting from poor interpersonal skills. After receiving consultation, the leaders became aware of the cultural dynamics operating within the group. The Native American client was encouraged to participate at her own pace, when and however she felt comfortable; relationship building was discussed in group as varying by ethnic heritage. This resulted in a productive interchange about cultural behavior patterns and frequent misinterpretations made by members of other ethnic groups.

Ethnic cultures frequently have traditions of group celebration of significant events and rites of passage. Due to this heritage, some ethnic clients may comfortably accept a group therapeutic focus if the symbolic nature of group experience is enhanced. Framing group treatment as a rite of passage to enable members to develop new roles or acquire new skills may enable ethnic clients to relate the experience to familiar customs. Adding aspects of ethnic group ritual, such as food, music, and an opening prayer or customary greeting may also enhance the comfort level of participants. Issues of heterogeneity versus homogeneity should be deliberately decided in the planning of groups. A homogenous group can easily incorporate rituals of the ethnic heritage all members share. However, a group with persons from diverse ethnic backgrounds may have difficulty coalescing and finding common methods of communicating and relating value differentials. One method to encourage connection may be trying out a variety of ethnic customs and behaviors on a rotational basis. This would give all group members more knowledge of various ethnic traditions and enable them to develop comfort in a multi-cultural context.

A mixed ethnic group offers an opportunity for group members to address issues of cultural diversity and to experience cultural practices different than their own. This will enable members to enrich their ethnic consciousness and to develop a group culture that encourages the bicultural adaptation of members.

In some ethnic communities, traditional healing methods have been revitalized to serve the needs of clients. Ho'oponopono is a Hawaiian conflict resolution process used with an extended family network when conflict between two members cannot be resolved (Ito, 1985). This technique was re-vitalized by a children's center using input from elder Hawaiians. It has been so successful that many other Hawaiian human service agencies now use this method. This is a good illustration of how indigenous ritualistic methods can resolve interpersonal problems.While typically used with a natural family group, they can easily be applied to a formed group.

## GROUP AS A MICROCOSM OF SOCIETY

A freely interactive group will develop into a social microcosm of its participants (Yalom, 1985). Members will interact with each other as they behave toward other people in their social sphere. The social sphere of all citizens in the U.S. includes discrimination and oppression of ethnic and minority groups. All group members have values and opinions about persons of minority status.

When a therapeutic group is composed of persons from a variety of ethnic backgrounds, issues of prejudice and bias frequently occur. If group members and leaders are of different ethnic backgrounds, the power relationships of society are re-enacted dynamically (Tsui & Schultz, 1988). If leaders are Caucasian and members are minorities of color, the tensions experienced by minority members in the larger society may be projected upon the leaders. Minorities may also disqualify leaders of a different race or ethnic background as too unlike them to understand their issues. In the intimate contact of therapeutic groups, confrontation can be misinterpreted as racially based and a form of discrimination. Stereotyping, scapegoating and polarization can easily occur.

To facilitate a positive multi-cultural environment, explicit discussion of feeling of bias and prejudice are necessary. Group leaders must be aware of their personal feelings of racism and prejudice in order to enable group members to discuss these volatile issues. Leaders must also model appropriate behaviors of respect and acceptance of individual difference. It is helpful for leaders to acknowledge the interplay between minority client's cultural heritage and the realities of the culturally diverse society in which they live (Tsui & Schultz, 1988). In this way, the multi-cultural awareness of group members can be enhanced. Participants learn to identify their own cultural bias, and hopefully reduce their prejudicial attitudes and behaviors.

## INTERVENTION STRATEGIES

Due to their unique cultural heritage and family structure, ethnic clients will experience therapeutic groups differently than members of the dominant culture. The group dynamics and culture which develops in a group with members from various ethnic backgrounds will be quite different than a group whose members all share the same ethnic heritage. The ethnic group experience can be a powerful healing experience when group leaders planfully utilize ethnic cultural dynamics.

To maximize the healing potential of multi-ethnic groups, leaders must develop a transcultural therapeutic perspective. This involves developing a personal comfort level with a variety of lifestyles, methods of verbal and nonverbal communication and culturally based emotive patterns. Leaders must communicate their respect for and value of the ethnic heritage of clients and encourage clients to share these values. Enabling clients to teach each other about their culture, unique communication styles, values and traditions will facilitate this process. By modeling an attitude of interest and willingness to learn about other cultures, leaders can support client self-esteem and build pride in their cultural backgrounds. In a society which devalues cultural difference, ethnic and minority group members often internalize a negative sense of self. Building a positive cultural identity is an important part of transcultural therapeutic work.

Another goal for leaders of therapeutic groups is to facilitate client bicultural skills. Living in a dominant Anglo-Euro-Caucasian society that has, until recently, prided itself on being a "melting pot," ethnic clients must have the necessary skills to negotiate a culture foreign to their own. In the open group climate previously described, leaders can use issues of cultural miscommunication and misinterpretation to teach clients new relationship skills. Role-plays between persons of different ethnic background can be used to teach and illustrate more facilitative communication and appropriate methods of expressing emotions and accomplishing tasks.

The goals of multi-ethnic groups are larger than solely facilitating solutions to clients problems. The group process becomes a vehicle for developing multi-cultural relationships and communication

skills. Clients can become comfortable in interpersonal relationships with persons from a wide variety of ethnic backgrounds. They
also learn about their personal bias and prejudice as well as their
tendency to misinterpret culturally different people due to a lack of
understanding of cultural behavior patterns and values.

The multi-ethnic therapy group can become a laboratory for
learning about cultural differences and appreciation of the varieties
of human expression and lifestyles. This can become as much a
learning experience for the group leaders as for the clients. Using
these approaches and techniques, social workers will become more
able to work with clients from a multitude of cultures and ethnic
backgrounds.

## CONCLUSION

Therapeutic groups whose members are culturally diverse have
unique dynamics. The comfort level of clients with a group format
will vary by ethnic heritage, as will the nature of their transference
patterns. Strained inter-group relations may occur as the group
comes to mirror societal patterns. Clinicians must enable group
members to explore their personal feelings toward cultural diversity
and to develop skills in cross-cultural communication and relation-
ship-building. Multi-ethnic groups are opportunities to develop bicultural skills as well as to raise ethnic consciousness. This type of
therapeutic work requires social workers to address their own personal reactions to ethnicity as well as to model respectful and effective cross-cultural relationships.

## REFERENCES

Ashby, M. R., Gilchrist, L. D. & Miramontez, A. (1987). Group treatment for
   sexually abused American Indian adolescents. *Social Work with Groups,*
   *10*(4), 21-32.
Chau, K. L. (1989). Sociocultural dissonance among ethnic minority populations.
   *Social Casework, 70,* 224-30.
Delgado, M. & Humm-Delgado, D. (1982). Natural support systems: Source of
   strength in Hispanic communities. *Social Work, 27*(1), 83-89.
Devore, W. & Schlesinger, E. (1987). Ethnic-sensitive social work practice. In

Minahan, A. et al. (Eds.), *Encyclopedia of Social Work*: Volume 1 (18th ed.). Silver Spring, MD: National Association of Social Workers.

Edwards, E. D. & Edwards, M. E. (1984). Group work practice with American Indians. *Social Work with Groups*, 7(3), 7-21.

Goldberg, A., Kestenbaum, S. & Shebar, V. (1987). Jerusalem, Arabs and Jews: What can group work offer? *Social Work with Groups*, 10(1), 73-83.

Granger, J. M. & Portner, D. L. (1985). Ethnic- and gender-sensitive social work practice. *Journal of Social Work Education*, 21(1), 38-47.

Hopps, J. G. (1982). Oppression based on color. *Social Work*, 27(1), 3-5.

Ito, K. L. (1985). Ho'oponopono, "to make right": Hawaiian conflict resolution and metaphor in the construction of a family therapy. *Culture, medicine & Psychiatry*, 9, 201-217.

Lee, P. C., Juan, G. & Hom, A. B. (1984). Group work practice with Asian clients: A socio-cultural approach. *Social Work with Groups*, 7(3), 37-48.

Lum, D. (1982). Toward a framework for social work practice with minorities. *Social Work*, 27(3), 244-249.

Manson, S. M., Walker, R. D. & Kivlahan, D. R. (1987). Psychiatric assessment and treatment of American Indians and Alaska Natives. *Hospital and Community Psychiatry*, 38, 165-173.

Norton, D. (1978). The dual perspective. In Norton, D. (Ed.), *The Dual Perspective: Inclusion of Ethnic Minority Content in Social Work Curriculum*. New York: Council on Social Work Education.

Tsui, P. & Schultz, G. L. (1988). Ethnic factors in group process: Cultural dynamics in multi-ethnic group therapy groups. *American Journal of Orthopsychiatry Bulletin*, 58(1), 136-142.

Yalom, I. D. (1985). *The theory and practice of group psychotherapy* (3rd ed.). New York: Basic Books, Inc.

# Managing Biculturalism at the Workplace:
# A Group Approach

## Nan Van Den Bergh

**SUMMARY.** America's workforce is becoming increasingly diverse as is witnessed by the fact that 75% of all new entrants to the labor force during the 1990s will be ethnic minorities and women. The successful integration of diverse employees into the workforce can be enhanced by using groups to facilitate the dual socialization process involved in developing a bicultural identity. Examples of four foci for workplace groups which can enhance biculturalism are shared. Developing workplace groups which enhance diversity increases bicultural employees' sense of belonging to the organization, which generates a more loyal and productive workforce.

## BICULTURAL TRENDS IN THE WORKFORCE

The face of America's workforce is changing. At present, only 46% of those employed are white males and by the year 1990, 75% of those entering the workforce will be ethnic minorities and women (Copeland, 1988a, p. 52). The growth of females and people of color within the workplace is particularly significant since during the last decade of this century there will be a shrinking labor pool, noted by 4 to 5 million fewer workers in 1990 than in 1980. This phenomenon is based upon the "baby bust" outcome of zero population growth trends. Additionally, during the 1990s, the percentage of ethnic minorities in the population will grow seven times faster than whites. In California, the percentage of whites will decrease from 64% to 48% by 2010 and in 2020, the majority of entry level workers in California will be Hispanic. At that time, English

Nan Van Den Bergh, PhD, is Director, Staff and Faculty Service Center, University of California, Los Angeles.

will become the second language for the majority of Californians (Copeland, 1988b, p. 52). Most poignantly, it is crucial to understand that during the Twenty-first century whites will acquire minority status within the United States, which is due in part to the fact that two-thirds of all global migration is into this country.

A conceptual framework prescriptive for considering how to manage diversity is biculturalism. That paradigm suggests that exposure to several cultures can be additive in the sense that an individual will maximize his/her coping mechanisms to be comfortable both with the dominant culture and one's own ethnic heritage (Kitano, 1980, p. 29). To become bicultural, an individual must engage in a dual socialization process. One acquires values, beliefs, communication and behavioral styles from a culture of origin as well as becoming exposed to the same dynamics of a majority culture. An ethnic minority will have success in becoming bicultural to the extent that crucial information and skills needed for negotiating the mainstream culture are provided, commensurate with receiving affirmation for the basic values, beliefs and behavioral styles of one's minority culture (de Anda, 1984, p. 107).

The implications of biculturalism for the workplace are as follows. For an ethnic minority to be a fully contributing member of an organization, he/she needs to be socialized into the "ways of being" for that workplace culture. This would include learning both written and unwritten rules for success including dress codes, preferred communication styles, how to take advantage of career development programs, ways to build both professional and personal support networks as well as how to establish a mentor relationship. If a minority was not able to adequately become socialized into a workplace culture (which for the most part will reflect mainstream values and beliefs) then sociocultural dissonance can arise. This concept relates to the stress, strain and incongruence which can occur for an individual attempting to belong to differing cultures (Chau, 1989, p. 221).

The individual experiencing sociocultural dissonance is caught in a dialectical process with two competing demands — maintenance of core beliefs, values and behavioral styles contrasted with adopting new and potentially conflictual attitudes and behaviors. For example, a minority may have culture of origin values such that deference toward others and deliberation in decision-making are valued. However, this person may join a work group which values brainstorming and assertiveness in presenting ideas. An obvious conflict exists which could deter the employee from being fully productive. However, if biculturalism and diversity are valued, conflict can be averted. First, the work group could explain their communication process and provide coaching as well as support for the ethnic employee to try out the process. Second, members of the work group could accommodate the ethnic employee by specifically drawing out his or her ideas during a "group think" brainstorming process.

The need for mutual accommodation and adaptation as a part of managing diversity underscores the ecological nature of promoting a bicultural workplace. An ecological process is operationalized as one whereby individuals are constantly interchanging with their environment. As people are changed by the contexts in which they live and work, so too are those environments altered in a process of continuous, reciprocal adaptation (Gitterman and Shulman, 1986). What the ecological model suggests, related to promoting biculturalism in the workplace, is that vehicles must be created which can facilitate ongoing reciprocal adaptation. The use of groups, both existing entities as well as those created specifically for diversity purposes, can be excellent vehicles for accommodating workplace biculturalism.

## *GROUP FOCI*
## *FOR MANAGING WORKPLACE BICULTURALISM*

Why are groups valuable in promoting workplace biculturalism and diversity? Basically, they allow for processes to occur which can both aid the individual as well as contribute to organizational effectiveness. Groups can nurture one's internal resources and strengths so that persons can cope with alienation, adapt to new roles, relate to conflicting values and norms as well as contribute to environmental change (Chau, 1989, p. 225). For ethnic minorities, participation within groups can serve the dual purposes of assisting with integration into mainstream society as well as reinforcing one's ethnic identity and pride. For the organization, groups focusing on ethnic diversity issues are a way to mobilize ideas, strengths and resources to create systems which allow diverse employees the opportunity to make productive contributions.

There are a number of foci which groups can have which could be helpful for both the individual and the organization in developing a dual, bicultural perspective. Groups could assist employees in adapting to the norms, values and rules of the workplace culture so that ethnic employees understand how to acquire opportunities and rewards. Also, groups can provide a linking and network function by encouraging varying ethnic groups to collaborate and build alliances. Also, ethnic employee groups can reinforce cultural pride and identity as well as serving to both protect and advocate for ethnic minority rights (adapted from Chau, 1989, p. 225). Within a workplace, all of the above noted foci would be appropriate organizing principles to consider when deliberating the purpose of an existing or proposed group for enhancing diversity.

### Guaranteeing Ethnic Group Rights

Let us consider examples of workplace groups which can be ethnic rights' guarantors. Within an academic environment, it is not unusual to find groups for particular ethnic faculty and staff, such as the Asian, Black, Native American or Hispanic Faculty and Staff Association. Usually, these groups serve as "watchdogs" for potential discrimination issues and are advocates for affirmative action recruitment and retention processes. Those functions are clearly related to group goals of initiating institutional change and advocating for equal opportunity. Ethnic faculty and staff associations can also undertake research assessing equity in salary and rank, which would be presented to higher education policy makers in order to influence institutional personnel policies. Such groups have also drafted position papers advocating for systemwide initiatives in promoting diversity within employment practices, advocating for the inclusion of diversity content within curricula as well as the need for a college or university to assert leadership within their larger community by supporting ethnic minority issues.

There is real power and influence that such groups can wield in protecting ethnic employee rights, as can be illustrated by two situations within an academic context. Recently, at a major university, a

Japanese faculty member was denied tenure. Organizations on campus representing Asian members of the academic community advocated on behalf of the assistant professor with the university's president. Ultimately, the faculty member was granted tenure.

Examples of ethnic groups advocating for employee rights and opportunities can also be shared by examining the activities of Jewish faculty associations at two major universities. One group exists for the primary purpose of assessing the impact of campus events on the quality of Jewish academic community life. An incident the group mobilized around related to the Jewish newspaper being set on fire and the director threatened. As a result, a committee was established to generate a strategy to be used in influencing the university's president to take a stand decrying the incident. At another university, a Jewish faculty group undertook proactive efforts to bring to their campus professors from other countries, such as Russia, whose academic freedom was being jeopardized.

The private sector is also witnessing the development of groups which have as their purpose advocacy for ethnic minority employees' concerns. For example, at Equitable Life Assurance, business resource groups meet with the firm's CEO in order to discuss company issues related to both minority and female employees. The CEO signs off on recommendations that the groups present which enhance diversity as well as organizational effectiveness. Then, a senior manager is assigned to implement the suggestions. On a quarterly basis the CEO asks for a report on progress being made with the diversity plans. At Avon, councils representing various minority groups provide both information and advice to top management on a regular basis. Each of the councils has a senior manager affiliated with it who has the means to "move diversity agendas" within the organization. At Proctor and Gamble, multicultural advisory teams exist which ongoingly monitor diversity activity within the firm and the extent to which ethnic minority employees become acclimated to the corporate culture.

The above examples from the private and public sector exemplify the ethnic rights focus which groups can provide in facilitating workplace biculturalism. A common thread throughout the examples was a group goal related to institutional change which could curtail discriminatory organizational behavior and provide equality of opportunity. Group tasks were of the advocacy and brokerage nature facilitating the ecological interchange between ethnic employees' needs and organizational response.

### Enhancing Bicultural Adaptation

Ethnic groups at the workplace can also take on a bicultural adaptation focus by helping minority members acclimate to the workplace majority culture. In providing adaptation functions, the group would assist in educational and socialization tasks which would teach the minority employee skills and knowledge requisite for succeeding within the organizational culture. There is historical precedent for the use of groups to assist in ethnic minority socialization as early social group work focused on assisting immigrants in their acculturation to American society. Those early group work efforts were aimed at assisting individuals in accommodating to industrialization as well as deterring any sense of social isolation while enhancing individuals' sense of self-worth (Middleman & Goldberg, 1987).

The provision of groups which allow for ethnic minority adaptation to the workplace is valuable not only for the employee but also for the organization, since the retention of valuable minority employees can be enhanced. It is important to realize that an organization loses money if minority employees do not stay. This is because it takes time for a firm to recoup the costs of training a new employee, in terms of the individual's productivity. This is true regardless of whether the minority is clerical, a service worker, managerial or professional in job-type. Hence, with the realities of an increasingly diverse workforce facing the United States, it becomes a "bottom-line" issue to conceptualize and implement programs which facilitate bicultural adaption and reduce sociocultural dissonance.

Initiatives related to providing groups which can enhance adaptation have begun, as can be witnessed by an endeavor undertaken by Proctor and Gamble. A study was done by that firm to determine how long it took for new hires to feel "joined-up," and the results indicated that gender and ethnicity were crucial explanatory variables. White males become acclimated most quickly while Black females took the longest time in order to feel "at home" with the company. As a result, an "on-boarding" process was developed which included the use of groups so that new ethnic and women employees could more quickly develop a sense of belonging. Additionally, a mentoring program was developed to raise the retention rate for Black and female managers and a Learning Task Force was established to determine the best learning experiences for the company's minority employees (Copeland, 1988d, p. 46). Also, at Security Pacific Bank, minority networks and support groups have been established for the purpose of encouraging both personal and professional growth within the firm's minority managers.

Groups for corporate V.I.P.s which will enhance ethnic minorities adaptation to the workforce have also been instituted to have top-down impact. For example, at Mobil, a special executive's group was created which has as its purpose the selection of women and minority employees who have potential to become high achievers within the firm. These individuals are taken from their staff functions and placed in capacities where they learn the oil business from the inside out, so that they can rise in managerial responsibility. A similar process exists at Digital Equipment Corporation. A top management "core group" was established as a safe place for managers to discuss how their feelings and attitudes about gender, racial and cultural differences affect the company decisions they make (Copeland, 1988d, p. 46).

The above examples from the private sector underscore the fact that enhancing biculturalism at the workplace is a reciprocal process requiring accommodation on the part of the organization as well as the individual. That is, the firms described above undertook actions requiring the investment of time and resources in order to optimize minority employees' participation within the organization. It is crucial to understand that a company/agency cannot carry on in a "business as usual" mode when confronted with diversity. Personnel practices may need to be altered allowing for flextime, maternity, paternity leave; benefits need to be offered which are complementary to varying forms of families and types of dependent care needs; and orientational as well as monitoring systems have to be established which give employees information on rules, norms and protocols. The payoff from investment in procedures which cause the organization to undergo change is greater employee commitment and commensurately, productivity enhancement.

Within academic communities, ethnic faculty and staff associations can also enhance adaptation for minorities. Perhaps the most distinguishable dual socialization function these groups play for faculty is observable when an academic joins the university from another country. By participating in an ethnic association, the individual will begin to acquire knowledge of how the campus operates as well as learning about ethnic resources within the larger community. To this extent, such groups play a key role in facilitating the minority member's dual socialization both into the academic community as well as into American culture.

In great part the development of biculturalism is made possible by creating translator, mediator and model relationships with ethnic colleagues. The above concepts, defined by de Anda (1984), relate to roles which can be played when assisting ethnics in adopting a dual socialization perspective. Within an academic context, a translator could be an accomplished ethnic professor who would impart his or her wisdom on how to navigate the dual socialization course in order to meet the behavioral demands of the academic majority culture. Mediators could be senior ethnic faculty, familiar with institutional policies and procedures, who would provide guidance as to the steps to be taken in meeting organizational expectations. A model could be an ethnic colleague, ostensibly comfortable and relatively successful in utilizing a bicultural behavioral repertoire who could assist the new faculty member in developing a style compatible with norms of both the ethnic and majority culture.

## Facilitating Ethnic Consciousness

A third focus workplace groups enhancing diversity can have is in facilitating ethnic pride and community building. The focus of these groups would be consciousness-raising, both for minorities and members of the majority workplace culture. Clearly, groups facilitating bicultural adaptation as were described previously, would have ethnic pride and consciousness-raising components since their focus is on maintaining one's own cultural roots while adopting attitudes and behaviors consonant with the majority culture. For example, it is common for Hispanic groups on an academic campus to sponsor or organize Cinco de Mayo celebrations. Similarly, Black History Month is usually promoted by the Black academic community on university campuses and will include cultural events as well as lectures celebrating Black contributions to society. In a related vein, associations representing Jewish employees have advocated for their group to be able to observe holidays such as Passover and Yom Kippur in order to maintain cultural traditions. When ethnic associations organize workplace events or observances of their cultural traditions, not only do group members benefit, but the organization gains by learning more about its employees. There are also obvious payoffs to the institution in terms of enhanced employee morale. Organizational support of ethnic pride celebrations creates a workplace environment where employees feel valued for their diversity which has obvious implications for employee loyalty and productivity.

The development of ethnic mutual aid and self-help groups plays a consciousness-raising/ethnic pride function as well as enhancing employee adaptation to the workplace. As was previously noted, several private sector firms which have clearly articulated corporate goals aimed at enhancing diversity have encouraged the development of support groups for ethnic employees (Copeland, 1988d). These groups are ethnic support and mutual aid networks which allow for the exchange of both instrumental assistance (how to get promoted) as well as affective support (how to maintain sanity!).

It may be that the successful management of workplace diversity can most effectively be achieved by encouraging the development of support and mutual aid groups amongst ethnic and female employees. A considerable amount of writing and research has been undertaken in defining the kind of help that mutual aid/support systems can provide (Gitterman and Shulman, 1986; Whittaker and Garbarino, 1983; Lee and Swenson, 1986; Hirsch, 1981; Gottlieb, 1981 and Froland and Pancoast, 1981). In articulating processes inherent within mutual aid groups, Gitterman and Shulman (1986) have noted several which have strong, positive implications for enhancing workplace diversity, including sharing information with colleagues/coworkers on organizational politics and resources, providing an opportunity to get support or develop strategy concerning discrimination issues, providing opportunities to solve problems or rehearse how to address a difficult situation, as well as offering the kind of love and support which is provided by being with "kindred spirits."

Offering mutual aid and self-help groups for minorities at the workplace also has preventive implications by providing an environment which could mediate sociocultural dissonance. Adapting a dual, bicultural perspective inherently causes an individual to experience periodic crises based on trying to reconcile conflictual or contradictory demands. An example might be the stress experienced by an ethnic employee coming from a cultural background which values cooperation, being placed in a work context where he or she is part of a team which values competition. The employee could either face failing at work or experiencing anxiety and depression by having to behave in a way contradictory to his/her values. By sharing their fears about this conflict within a support group, ethnic employees could acquire both empathy and some concrete suggestions on managing the situation, all of which could avert either a firing or voluntary termination. As Bertha Reynolds, activist and organizational social worker stated: "It is not hard to take help in a circle in which one feels sure of belonging . . . " (Reynolds, 1975, p. 10).

Consciousness-raising activities by ethnic groups at the workplace can also have an impact on the larger community. For example, the Latino Staff and Faculty Association of a major university recently sponsored a speech, given by President Bush, on the political and social implications of the growing Hispanic population within the country. This event was opened to the community in an effort to demonstrate the university's commitment to supporting biculturalism and diversity both within its own organization as well as within its service delivery area.

### Intergroup Cooperation

A fourth focus for ethnic minority groups in the workplace is the encouragement of inter-ethnic group acceptance and cooperation. There is real social change potential with this focus. If different ethnic groups can pursue joint ventures within an organization, then that camaraderie can be generalized to cooperation within the community at large. This may be the most exciting challenge incumbent with the development of an increasingly diverse workforce, as the workplace may become the venue where individuals learn how to accept differences. Basically, this could occur as people acquire more experience in dealing with those different from themselves. Since individuals stereotype those who are unfamiliar, then the propensity to be prejudicial in attitudes and discriminatory in behaviors could be reduced.

An example of inter-ethnic group collaboration at the workplace relates to the development of a diversity network within an academic environment. For several years a number of groups had independently been meeting and working on "diversity agendas" related to their role and function within the organization. At some point these groups began crossing paths and decided they should convene all parties who had been pursuing their own diversity activities. There were several positive outcomes from the initial collaborative meeting of those groups. First, individuals came to know each other better and acquired a better understanding of each others' roles within the organization. Second, a task force was created which was given the charge of designing criteria which were to be included in all diversity training conducted on the campus, regardless of who facilitated the learning experience. Hence, an outcome of that inter-ethnic group venture was the establishment of policy and procedures which helped to institutionalize diversity training within the organization.

The above example highlights how diversity work can take on the cast of planned change, in the organizational development sense. Because resistance is endemic to the change process, the creation of intergroup cooperation by ethnic group networking could ameliorate problems and facilitate goal accomplishment in an expeditious fashion.

## PROFESSIONAL ROLES
## WITH WORKPLACE DIVERSITY GROUPS

Having examined various ways in which workplace groups can support cultural diversity, it is appropriate to discuss the roles human service practitioners can play with those groups. Within the social work profession, most practitioners within workplace contexts would be providing employee assistance program services. As an EAP professional, one could not only engage in organizational development efforts aimed at enhancing workplace biculturalism and diversity, but also create important service delivery systems enhancing the EAP, such as the diversity network described below.

As a potential means for assisting ethnic employees with diversity problems, an internal EAP established a "diversity network." The purpose of that service delivery system was to identify peer support and mutual aid for employees experiencing diversity problems.

Providing peer support through the diversity network for ethnic employees was done in the following way. When an ethnic employee came to the EAP for assistance, if the individual's problem was such that he or she could benefit by speaking to another ethnic employee who had resolved a similar issue, a "peer supporter" was contacted. The peer was asked if he/she would be willing to meet the EAP client, on their own time, to discuss the issue. The phone number of the "peer supporter" was never given out without his/her prior approval. The two individuals could then meet over coffee or lunch and share their experiences. That process was utilized as an adjunct to the professional guidance and counseling provided to the troubled employee by the EAP professional, and was never the sole assistance an individual receives.

All potential "peer supporters" were provided training, as part of the diversity network group experience. Individuals volunteering to be part of the diversity network were taught three core helping skills: (1) empathetic listening, (2) reflection of feelings and (3) presentation of behavioral alternatives. They were admonished not to provide specific advice, nor to offer platitudes such as "count your blessings."

The development of self-help and mutual aid diversity networks has obvious win-win potential both for the EAP and for an organization's ethnic employees. There are additional ways that the EAP and workplace ethnic groups can mutually be advantaged by working with each other. For example, the EAP can offer advisory assistance to ethnic work groups by clarifying organizational policies and procedures related to affirmative action and sexual harassment. In that same vein, the EAP can be a linking agent by clarifying resources available to the ethnic group from varying organizational units, as well as identifying other groups interested in similar goals. The EAP can also gain immeasurably by collaborating with workplace ethnic groups since its knowledge of ethnic community resources can be expanded. This information would then enhance the assistance EAP professionals could provide to ethnic clientele using its services.

## CONCLUSION

Answering the challenge of how to manage an increasingly diverse workforce can be facilitated by utilizing groups within the workplace that promote biculturalism. Since the bicultural model is inherently additive, that is, it acknowledges one as being facile within both a dominant and an ethnic heritage culture, then promoting biculturalism suggests growth, expansion and opportunity. Ethnically diverse employees become assets rather than liabilities since they have multiple perspectives which can be utilized in solving problems.

Enhancing biculturalism at the workplace through groups means providing opportunities for ethnic minorities to create mutual aid/ social support networks as well as establishing groups focused on specific knowledge and skill-building to enhance their acclimation to the organizational culture. Providing these offerings will enhance ethnic employees' adaptation to the workforce, encourage their pursuit of opportunities, promote cultural pride, enrich the organizational culture and provide a sense of community and wellbeing. In addition, the organization will become more flexible in accommodating diversity by allowing for greater behavioral repertoires in communication styles and problem solving/decision making processes. Additionally, workplace norms on what constitutes success and how to achieve it will need to expand so as to accommodate values of sharing, cooperation and building relationships as opposed to exclusively promoting competition, power-over and conquest as priorities.

The Chinese symbol for crisis includes two concepts: danger and opportunity. Somehow that configuration seems apropos for the reality facing organizations in managing diversity. The danger lies in doing nothing, but reacting to problems created by tension, conflict and terminations. On the other hand, opportunity exists in actively reaching out to capitalize on differences; seeing them as resources capable of enriching an organization's future.

# REFERENCES

Chau, K. (1989). Sociocultural dissonance among ethnic minority populations. *Social Casework*, April, 224-230.

Copeland, L. (1988a). Learning to manage a multicultural workforce. *Training*, May, 52-56.

Copeland, L. (1988b). Making the most of cultural differences. *Personnel*, June, 52-56.

Copeland, L. (1988c). Valuing diversity, Part 1, Video Discussion Guide. *Managing Differences*, San Francisco: Copeland Griggs Productions.

Copeland, L. (1988d). Pioneers and champions of change. *Personnel*, July 44-48.

Coyle, G. (1979). *Social Processes in Organized Groups*. Hebron, CT: Practitioner's Press.

deAnda, D. (1984). Bicultural socialization: Factors affecting the minority experience. *Social Work*, March/April, 101-105.

Froland, C., Pancoast, D., Chapman, N., Kinboko,P. (1981). *Helping Networks and Human Services*. Beverly Hills: Sage Publications, 1981.

Gitterman, D. and Shulman, L. (1986). The life model, mutual aid and the mediating function. In A. Gitterman and L. Shulman (Eds.), *Mutual Aid Groups and the Life Cycle*. (pp. 3-22). Itaska, IL: Peacock Publishers.

Gottlieb, B. (1981). Preventive interventions involving social networks and social support. In B. Gottlieb (Ed.), *Social Networks and Social Support* (pp. 201-232). Beverly Hills: Sage Publications.

Hirsch, B. (1981). Social networks and the coping process: Creating personal communities. In B. Gottlieb (Ed.), *Social Networks and Social Support* (pp. 149-170). Beverly Hills: Sage Publications.

Kitano, H. (1980). *Race Relations*. Englewood Cliffs, NJ: Prentice-Hall Inc.

Lee, J. and Swenson, C. (1986). The concept of mutual aid. In A. Gitterman and L. Shulman, *Mutual Aid Groups and the Life Cycle*. (pp. 361-380) Itasca, IL: Peacock Publishers.

Middleman, R. and Goldberg, G. (1987). Social Work Practice with Groups. In A. Minahan et al. (Eds.). *Encyclopedia of Social Work*, Eighteenth Edition, v. 2, (pp. 714-729). Englewood Cliffs, NJ: N.A.S.W.

Toffler, A. (1971). *Future Shock*. New York: Bantam Books.

Whittaker, J. and Garbarino, J. (1983). *Social Support Networks*. New York: Aldine Press.

# Group Work with Families:
# A Multicultural Perspective

Joseph D. Anderson

**SUMMARY.** Family practice is a special case of social work with groups. This practice especially requires an ethnic and multicultural perspective. Such a framework is presented in this paper with focus on group work with families in Singapore. Singapore is an economically developed East Asian nation populated predominately by three ethnic groups: Chinese, Malay, and Indian. These groups have experienced a wider culture in transition, affecting their family group culture. Through use of the sensitizing conceptual frameworks of family cultural reality and value orientation theory, this paper presents a multicultural perspective and applies it to group work with families in Singapore. The framework used is deemed applicable to practice with the family and other small groups in similar multicultural contexts wherein members experience the effects of swift social change.

Family practice is a special case of social work with groups. The family practitioner continually focuses upon the family as a group. All assessment and intervention, whether the service is delivered primarily through work with individuals, formed small groups, or a particular family system, targets on the family as a group system. This focus on the family as a group is the central aspect of practice in Eastern Societies such as Singapore. This article presents and applies a framework for aspects of multicultural group work with families that the author found useful for studying and teaching practice in Singapore. This framework seems promising for its applica-

Joseph D. Anderson, DSW, ACSW, is Senior Visiting Teaching Fellow, National University of Singapore.

bility to family and other small group practice in similar multicultural contexts.

Singapore is an independent republic of over two- and one-half million people, located at the tip of Malaysia Peninsula. Of this population, approximately 76% are Chinese, 15% are Malays, 7% Indians, and 2% other ethnic groups (such as Eurasian, Arab, Thai, Sri Lakan, Filipino, and various Europeans). In a political democracy with strong centralized planning, Singapore's economy expanded greatly within the last two decades. The per capita income is now second only to Japan in Asia.

Within its multicultural and multi-ethnic diversity, Singaporeans share a national identity and pride and the value of the family group as the basic unit for defining the individual and the society. This ethnic and multicultural development is reflected in official policy wherein the National Anthem is in the Malay language, and all students are educated in English yet required to take either Mandarin, Tamil, or Malay as a second language. In addition, the Chinese dialects of Cantonese and Hokkien, Malay, and for the Indians, Tamil, are still very often spoken at home.

## SINGAPORE FAMILY GROUPS
## IN CULTURAL TRANSITION

A decade ago, Eddie Kuo and Aline Wong (1979) depicted the Singapore family as a system in cultural transition in a rapidly changing, modernizing society. Their study noted the policies and programs by which the government attempted to manage this change toward "modernization by design." Government policy promotes the family unit as the major group for blending the traditional and modern in its development of members' knowledge, values and skills. As Kuo and Wong hypothesized, the family in this situation is "expected to serve an important role as a social unit in which the resources of individual members are to be pooled together for the common family good, which stated bluntly, means an improved material living standard" (p. 11). In other words, the family group is viewed as primarily responsible for its economic security and mobility. At the same time, the family is expected to preserve the traditional values while bearing the primary responsibility of instilling the virtues of economic productivity. This task requires continuous adaptive changes in the family group's structure and values in order to function adequately in a more advanced industrial society.

In his earlier study of low income Singaporean families in public housing, Riaz Hassan (1977) identified this shift in values, found prevalent today. The adaptation to swift socio-economic change has resulted in family groups developing what he calls a "transitional syndrome." The transitional syndrome is defined as " a set of psychological and behavioral orientations such as receptiveness to change. Social mobility, economic rationality, achievement, materialism, individualism, acquisitiveness and above all, an orientation that emphasizes change and progress as a highly desirable goal" (p.17).

Group work with families in Singapore needs to understand the family group in the context of this ecology of change. In the process of bearing the weight and absorbing the shocks of personal and social change, the modern Singaporean family needs a vast array of resources. The quantity of these resources, however, is not enough. These resources must be ecologically relevant. This is, they must target on the priority problems that families as a group and their individual members face in their cultural context. When families are undergoing such acculturation as those in Singapore, the problems are primarily those of cultural transition—such as the transitional conflicts among family members and between families and the larger sociocultural world. Family group culture, therefore, is the focus from which to begin the therapeutic process (Papajohn and Spiegel, 1975). The foundation for this practice is a multicultural perspective which attends to the value orientations and conflicts that comprise family group culture.

## FAMILY CULTURAL REALITY

Milton Gordon (1973), in his penetrating analysis of the relationship among human nature, social class and ethnicity, suggests that the point at which social class and ethnic group membership intersect be characterized as "ethclass." Gordon initially, and more recently Wynette Devore and E. G. Schlesinger (1981), used the ethclass concept to explain the role that social class membership plays in defining the basic conditions of life at the same time accounting for differences between groups at the same social class level. They explain these differences largely by ethnic group membership.

This intersect of ethnicity and social class, or ethclass, when incorporated with generation and the influence of the mainstream culture, converge to generate identifiable values, norms, and behaviors. These value and norm dispositions, and the behaviors which flow from them, constitute "family cultural reality." Thus, family cultural dispositions on such matters as rules for appropriate child-rearing practices or proper care for the elderly, though in large measure related to social-class membership, are often affected by ethnicity and generational experiences as well as by transactions with the wider culture. The concept of cultural reality in the Singapore context is depicted in Figure 1.1 (as adapted from Devore and Schlesinger, 1981).

The ethclass intersect of social class, ethnicity, and generation creates the "social space" of the family's cultural reality and its particular "world view." The vertical axis represents ethnicity and the associated sense of peoplehood. Ethnicity consists of the sharing of a common heritage in terms of race, religion, national origin, and/or language. This vertical axis of ethnicity stresses the fact that it is a component of social life at all social class levels.

Social class is represented by the horizontal axis. This reflects a combination of occupation, education, and income. Social class also is a component of social life for all ethnic groups.

The generational axis (the dotted, slanted line) reflects the socio-historical context. This especially includes the intra-generational and inter-generational life experiences of family members.

The circles represent the cultural reality (or ethclass/generation-in-action) as it affects individual and family group world views and behavior. This cultural reality suggests that as social class intersects with ethnicity and generational history in a given society, an unique configuration is formed for families and their members.

A recent exploratory study (Vigmesha and Minai, 1988) of family socialization values in Singapore tends to support this framework. This study reveals a core of socialization values shared by most Singaporean families: discipline/obedience, honesty/integrity,

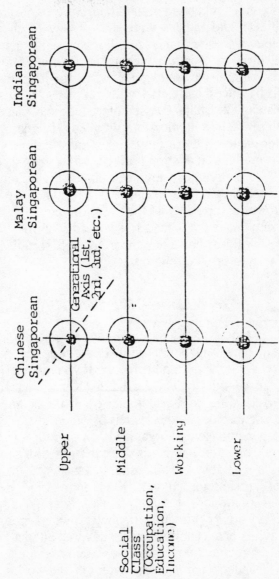

FIGURE 1.1. Family Cultural Reality in Singapore

filial piety, diligence, and compassion. While these values tended to cross ethnic and class groups, there were significant differences. The Chinese and Indians were more likely to choose these core values than were the Malays and Eurasians. Even more significant were the differences in respondents' ideal values for their children's socialization and the sources identified for learning these values. These differences correlated with religion, ethnicity, and class. Muslims and Christians stressed more religious piety. Middle class respondents, across ethnic groups ranked cleverness, independence and assertiveness significantly higher and filial piety lower. While parents were viewed as strong sources of teaching these ideal values to children, the schools were even ranked higher on this source by Chinese and Indian respondents. Malays ranked the school significantly lower and parents as first and foremost. This research suggests that Singaporeans tend to share an identification of core socialization values; however, there are still significant differences related to ethclass and religion.

## VALUE ORIENTATIONS

Another aspect of the multicultural perspective for group work with families in Singapore is *value orientation* theory. Value orientation theory evolved from the theory of variations in cultural values first proposed by Clyde Kluckhohn (Kluckhohn and Strodbeck, 1961). According to Kluckhohn, orientations are distinguished from concrete values by their levels of generality: "A value orientation in a generalized and organized conception, influencing behavior of time, of nature, of man's place in it, of man's relation to man, and of the desirable and undesirable aspects of man-environment and inter-human transactions" (Kluckhohn, 1951, p. 14).

Value orientations have three significant qualities (Spiegel, 1983). They are: (1) directional — they provide a program for selecting behaviors between more or less favored alternatives; (2) cognitive — they provide a conceptual world view through which people filter their understanding of the nature of the world and human affairs; and (3) affective — they are invested with strong emotional themes which contribute to people and social systems, such as families, becoming so resistant to change.

In social work, John Spiegel (1983) has classified value orientations to distinguish among ethnic family group cultures. His classification is based on the following assumptions, consistent with the propositions of Kluckhohn:

1. There are a limited number of common human problems for which all people in all places must find solutions. These are:
   a. Time—the temporal focus of human life
   b. Activity—the preferred pattern of action in interpersonal relations
   c. Human Relations—the preferred way of relating in groups
   d. Person—Nature Relationship—the way people relate to the natural or supernatural environment
   e. Basic Nature of Human Beings—the attitudes held about the innate good or evil in human nature and behavior.

2. Although there is variability in the solutions to these problems, this diversity is neither limitless nor random but occurs within a range of three possible solutions, or general value orientations, for each of these problems.
   a. Time—Past, Present, Future
   b. Activity—Doing, Being, Becoming
   c. Human Relations—Autonomy, Interdependency, Hierarchy
   d. Person-Nature—Harmony, Mastery, Subjugation
   e. Basic Nature of Human Beings—Neutral/Mixed, Good, Evil

3. All possible solutions are in varying degrees present in the total structure of every culture, and every culture will be characterized not only by a dominant profile of first-order choices but also by substitute second- and third-order choices. Differences among various cultures are based on the pattern of preferences for each of these solutions in a dominant-substitute profile of values.

In the process of sociocultural change, second-order choices may move into the first order and *vice versa*. This shifting in value orientation is often the key to understanding generational problems and conflicts, such as those among parents and children or aspects of marital difficulties. For example, many families experience differential rates of cultural transition among their subsystems. This tends inevitably to lead to transitional value conflicts. Similarly, cultural lag (Ogburn, 1964) suggests that the dominant culture may shift value orientations before other segments of the society (e.g., some ethnic families who are influenced greatly by their subcultural values). This also tends inevitably to lead to transitional conflicts.

Thus, value orientation theory can aid the identification of significant aspects of the problems and conflicts for families in cultural transition. At the general level of social work practice, this theory can be applied in the assessment of problems in the transactions between the family and the wider ecological context, within the family group itself, and within its inter-generational processes. It also can illuminate ethnic differences in families. At the more specific level, the theory provides direction for bicultural practice. There are at least four issues of bicultural group work with families where value orientation theory can instruct practice:

1. Differences between Western practice theory for group work with families and the cultural context families serve;
2. Differences between the practitioner's ethnic and cultural perspective and the family's;
3. Differences between the ethnic values of family groups whom social workers serve;
4. Differences between class values, e.g., the subculture of families in poverty.

Table 1.1 is an example of how value orientation theory helps to illuminate and understand these differences with Singaporean families. The table provides a comparative analysis of the different "world views" impacting on group work with families in Singapore. These include the dominant society's modern middle-class value orientations; the more traditional Chinese, Malay and Indian ethnic values; the probable value orientation for these families with low incomes or in poverty; and the perspective of Western theory for family group practice.

In modern industrialized societies, middle-class value orientations tend to dominate in the culture-at-large. The mainstream culture in Singapore appears in transition toward this middle-class dominance. Thus, the basis for much of the cultural conflicts can be seen as the confrontation of difference between these dominating middle-class value orientations and the more traditional ethnic world views in this bicultural context. Within individuals and family groups there are points of congruence and incongruence among class and ethnic values.

Table 1.1 identifies the profile of Singaporean middle-class values in the first column. In relation to Time, the first-order value is a future orientation. The middle class family group tends to plan the family and the educational and economic careers of its members. Family resources are prioritized toward the achievement of social mobility and progress. This future orientation places importance on novelty and transience. The new is conceived as better than the old — new flat, new car, newest fashion, etc. Often, youth are more valued than the aged as they represent the future rather than the "outmoded" past.

The second-order Time value is the present. The present is valued primarily as a respite from the stresses of preparing for and ensuring a planned future. It is a time for play and relaxation. Here too, for the middle class the future often invades the present. Families and individuals interrupt their play to prepare for school, an early business meeting, and so on. The past is a distant third-order value. The middle class in Singapore, as in all modernized and industrialized societies, tend to be pro-progress and anti-tradition. Past traditions take on more importance primarily in family and ethnic rituals and in the fears that there is a loss of values during transition toward the new.

In relation to Activity, the first-order value orientation is doing. The emphasis is on competitiveness, meritocracy, what one produces, and the striving through accomplishments for upward mobility. Strangers meeting each other likely begin their relationship with the question: "What do you do?" This value includes strong sanctions for controlling feelings in behalf of task-accomplishment. The second-order value is a becoming orientation. Here, the priority is upon developing one's potentials, especially through education and training. A distant third-order is being, which promotes more spontaneous and authentic experiencing of feelings. These feelings, as

TABLE 1.1 Comparison of Value Orientation Profiles

| | Singaporean Middle Class | Chinese-Singaporean | Malay-Singaporean |
|---|---|---|---|
| Time | Future>Present>Past | Future>Past>Present | Present>Past>Future |
| Activity | Doing>Becoming>Being | Doing>Becoming>Being | Being>Becoming>Doing |
| Human Relations | Autonomy>Interdependency>Hierarchy | Hierarchy>Interdependency>Autonomy | Interdependency>Hierarchy>Autonomy |
| Person-Nature Relationship | Mastery>Subjugation>Harmony | Subjugation>Mastery>Harmony | Harmony>Subjugation>Mastery |
| Basic Nature of Human Beings | Neutral>Evil>Good | Neutral>Good>Evil | Good>Mixed>Evil |

noted above, are often viewed as obstacles to doing and becoming which are best controlled rather than expressed.

In Human Relations, the middle-class first-order value orientation is autonomy. The emphasis on the future for social mobility and on competitiveness for doing by necessity promotes over interdependence. For instance, there are strong forces to consider one's own and one's children's future careers over other aspects of family responsibility. A second-order value is the interdependency orientation. After autonomy and to counterbalance too much self-serving liberty, there is a tendency toward responsibility to the group. The middle-class pull toward autonomy and among from interdependence appears as one of the most pervasive aspects of cultural con-

| Indian–Singaporean | Singaporean Lower Class | Western Family Practice Theory |
|---|---|---|
| Past>Future>Present | Present>Past>Future | Future>Prescent>Past |
| >Becoming>Doing>Being | Being>Doing>Becoming | Doing>Becoming>Being |
| Hierarchy>Interdependency>Autonomy | Hierarchy>Autonomy>Interdependency | Autonomy>Interdependency>Hierarchy |
| Subjugation>Harmony>Mastery | Subjugation>Mastery>Harmony | Mastery>Subjugation>Harmony |
| Mixed>Good>Evil | Evil>Mixed>Good | Neutral>Good>Evil |

flicts for the Singaporean family. It is an area in which class confronts ethnicity and the future confronts the past in such problems as parent-adolescent and other inter-generational conflicts.[1] The third-order value is hierarchy. This orientation bases much of bureaucratic organization. It also tends to rise in priority in families and the wider society in the face of group crises.

In Person-Nature, the first-order is a mastery orientation. This value views all problems as solvable given an adequate technology and enough money. If problems persist and appear nonsolvable, the subjugation orientation, a second-order value, may gain more prominence. Here, problems are seen as part of nature, that some suffering is unavoidable, and that one must surrender to these facts

of nature or appeal to a higher being. The third-order harmony orientation is much further removed from the dichotomous mastery
and subjugation values. This assumes that there is not necessarily a
clash between humans and nature but that there are many forces at
work in both the heavens and on earth (e.g., gods, demons, spirits,
ghosts, etc.). Human problems arise when we are not balanced with
these sources of influence. While many people may secretly and
ethnically believe in some aspects of this orientation, harmony is
often conceived to be superstitious or magical and put down by the
mainstream middle class.

In Basic Nature of Human Beings, the middle-class first-order
value is the neutral orientation. People are conceived primarily as
blank slates who can be shaped into functional individuals. The
emphasis is on moral pragmatism and the establishment of laws to
mold people's behavior. The second-order evil orientation values
the control of human behavior for fear of unbridled instincts which
are assumed to be more animalistic and barbarian. The third-order
is good-but-corruptible. To the middle class this value is often
viewed as a romantic ideal that is not appropriate pragmatically.

## IMPLICATIONS FOR GROUP WORK WITH FAMILIES
## IN SINGAPORE

A comparative analysis of Table 1.1 reveals some major points of
congruence and discongruence in the bicultural realities of Singaporean families. First, there is a direct parallel between the Singaporean middle-class world view and that of western family group
practice theory. There is some congruence, too, between the Chinese ethnic group[2] and the middle class and Western practice theory
values—especially strong in the activity dimension. However, the
differences are significant. One might expect special culturally-re-
lated problems for first- and second-generation middle-class Chinese families, for instance, in their stronger value of the past, in
their weaker value of autonomy, and in the definition of hierarchial
power in family systems. Socially mobile Malay families appear to
experience even more tensions among these value orientations and
need special adaptations of the theoretical approaches for group
work with families. Their ethnic reality might confront special bi-

cultural conflicts in most of the dimensions of these value orientations, especially for integrating the future, doing, autonomy, and mastery orientations with the present, being, interdependency, and harmony ones which seem to be so much a part of their more village-based cultural heritage and their religious traditions. Indian families may meet special challenges in the tension between autonomy and their value of hierarchical family relationships and between the tendency to subjugate to nature in the face of problems and the value of mastery in problem-solving. The Singaporean poor, regardless of ethnicity, appear to be a separate distinct subculture. Low income and poor families, with these more subcultural value orientations, face grave difficulties, in addition to the serious lack of opportunity and resources, in preparing members for social mobility in the wider culture. They need empowering group approaches especially adapted to altering such bicultural incongruencies.

The multicultural perspective for understanding families in cultural transition has a number of implications for the general approaches to group work with families. First, an assessment of family culture as it affects the family's resources and rules determines the most appropriate approaches for providing family group services. For example, life education groups are designed primarily for helping families clarify their values and gain knowledge and skills for the purpose of preventing more chronic problems in marital disorders, parent-child relationships, and so on. These seem especially appropriate for working and middle class Chinese and Indians. Family group problem-solving approaches help families deal with specific problems and crises through some attention to how the family's current interactional patterns create both obstacles and resources for problem resolution. These fit better traditional Malay and Chinese. Family group therapy approaches target on those families whose overall system needs changed, including family cultural value changes. The theoretical models for these clinical approaches, primarily derived from the Western perspective, need special adaptation for relevance to the bicultural (at least) ethnic realities of Singaporean families. While they may have more general validity in practice with second or third-generation middle class families across ethnic groups, they are not so directly appropriate to first-generation middle class families and would need to be adapted to account for more discrete Chinese, Malay, and Indian ethnic world views. They are even less relevant for working class and poor families from all these major ethnic groups.

Second, all group practice approaches and models require work with family values in family groups in cultural transition. Practitioners need to be especially sensitive to their own family values and the differences in family groups' ethclass values. The practice, regardless of approach and model, needs to respect value differences at the same time it aids families in groups to negotiate values that work for them. For instance, this suggests that practitioners do not impose their biases of what constitutes healthy family systems on the family group. Rather, the practitioner helps the family group share its family paradigm of a healthy family system, understand how its rituals for everyday life reflect such a world view and how its rules operate to regulate it, and consider whether these value orientations are what family members want—how they work or do not for the family as a group to achieve individual member's and the family system's goals.

Third, a prerequisite skill to any assessment and contact in social work multicultural practice with family groups is "tuning-in" (Anderson, 1988). Tuning-in is the skill of preliminary empathy in which the practitioner anticipates needs and themes in working with a family in terms of his or her own biases, values, and feelings and in terms of the family group and its various members' ecological "life space." This life space includes some knowledge and understanding of values and norms related to ethnicity, class, inter-generational experiences, and the likely relationship of these to the wider multicultural and mainstream society.

Any planning of approaches and models would derive from this tuning-in and the use of the multicultural perspective in assessment. This includes using approaches that begin where families are—in their own definition of needs and goals for service—and in the use of models and skills which are not too incompatible with their value orientation profile (e.g., emphasizing too much expression of feelings, promoting too much autonomy for adolescents, and so on).

Lastly, whatever the specific group approaches used, family practice in Singapore needs to help families as a group to develop consciousness of their own cultures and the variables influencing their transitional needs, stresses and/or problems. They need to increase their awareness of how their family culture, especially their ethnicity and traditions in transaction with such rapid personal and social changes, are a source of cohesion, identity, and strength as well as a source of strain, discordance, and strife. An important function of group work with families in cultural transition is developing their insight both into their own system and its transaction with the world at large. It is this insight which can promote their integrity and choice in determining the present and future strength of their family in preparing members to live fully in an ever-evolving multicultural world.

## CONCLUSION

This article presented a multicultural perspective for group work with families in Singapore. This multicultural perspective is especially useful for understanding cultural transitions and their effect on families in modernizing multicultural societies. Practice with families experiencing such cultural transition often needs to make aspects of family group culture the focus from which to begin any problem-solving process. This perspective for practice combines the concepts of social class, ethnicity, and generational history to illuminate and understand significant aspects of a family's cultural reality. This family group's "world view" in transaction with the dominant mainstream culture can also be examined through value orientation theory.

The concepts of the Singaporean family's traditional and transitional culture reality and its value orientation imply particular relevance for the general group work approaches. Using approaches discriminatively requires the practitioner to be attuned to the family's particular culture and its sources of strength and stress for the family as a group in adapting functionally to personal and social change. A multicultural framework, such as the one presented in this article, is especially pertinent to this practice. It also seems promising for such family and small group practice in other multicultural contexts.

## NOTES

1. The rise of the more individualistic value of autonomy over the social unit value of interdependence, for instance, is one of the major concerns of Singapore's government leaders. This has been labelled the problem of Western values contaminating Eastern traditions. For instance, Brig. Gen. Lee Hsien Loong [1988, p. 925] has written: "In the other Western industrial economies, . . . the erosion of the work ethnic and the breakup of the family have undermined social cohesion and economic productivity . . . We must ensure that our fundamental values, which place the welfare of society above that of the individual and help to contain social dissension and industrial unrest, are never eroded."

2. Sources of identifying these ethnic class values are: for Chinese (Chan, 1963; Fairbanks, Reischauer and Craig, 1965; Hsu, 1963; Hu, 1975; Murphy and Murphy, 1968; Shon and Ja, 1983; Yutang, 1942); for Indian (Balgopal, 1988; Desai and Coelho, 1980; Hsu, 1963; Murphy and Murphy, 1968; Ramakrishnan and Balgopal, 1985-86; Varma, 1980; Yutang, 1942; Zimmer, 1951); and for Malay (Alwi, 1962; Brown, 1969; Djamour, 1965; Hanna, 1966; Knappert, 1980).

## REFERENCES

Alwi, S.A. (1962). *Malay Customs and Traditions*. Singapore: Donald More.

Anderson, J. (1988). *Foundations of Social Work Practice*. New York: Springer.

Balgopal, P.R. (1988). Social Networks for Asian Indian Families. In *Ethnicity and Race: Critical Concepts in Social Work*. C. Jacobs and D.P. Bowles (Eds.). Silver Spring, MD: National Association of Social Workers.

Bowen, M. (1978). *Family Therapy in Clinical Practice*. New York: Aronson.

Brown, C.C. (1969). *Malay Sayings*. Singapore: Asian Pacific Press.

Chan, W.T. (1963). *A Source Book in Chinese Philosophy*. Princeton: Princeton University Press.

Desai, P.N. and Coelho, G.V. (1980). Indian Immigrants in America: Some Cultural Aspects of Psychological Adaptation. In *The New Ethnics*. P. Saran and E. Eames (Eds.). New York: Praeger.

Devore, W. and Schlesinger, E.G. (1981). *Ethnic-Sensitive Social Work Practice*. London: C.V. Mosby.

Djamour, J. (1965). *Malay Kinship and Marriage*, Rev. Ed. London: Athlone.

Fairbanks, J., Reischauer, E. and Craig, A. (1965). East Asian, the Modern Transformation. In *A History of East Asian Civilization II*. Tokyo: Charles E. Tuttle.

Gordon, M.M. (1973). *Human Nature, Class and Ethnicity*. London: Oxford University Press.

Hanna, W.A. (1966). *The Malays' Singapore*. New York: American University Field Staff.

Hassan, R. (1977). *A Study of Low Income Families in Public Housing*. Singapore: National University of Singapore Press.

Hsu, F. (1963). *Clan, Caste, and Club: A Comparative Study of Chinese, Hindu, and American Ways of Live*. Princeton: Van Nostrand.

Hu, H.C. (1975). The Chinese Concepts of Face. In *Personal Character and Cultural Milieu*. P.G. Haring (Ed.). Syracuse: Syracuse University Press.

Kluckhohn, C. (1951). Values and Value Orientations. In *Toward A General Theory of Action*. T. Parsons and E. Shils (Eds.). Cambridge: Harvard University Press.

Kluckhohn, F.R. and Stodtbeck, F.L. (1961). *Variations in Value Orientations*. Evanston, IL: Row, Peterson.

Knappert, J. (trans.) (1980). *Malay Myths and Legends*. Kuala Lumpur: Heinemann.

Kuo, E. and Wong, A. (1979). *The Family in Contemporary Singapore*. Singapore: National University of Singapore Press.

Lee, H.L. (1988). Statement. In C.Y. Lim and associates, *Policy Options for the Singapore Economy*. Singapore: McGraw-Hill.

Murphy, G. and Murphy, Le B. (Eds.) (1968). *Asian Psychology*. London: Basic Books.

Ogburn, W.F. (1964). *On Culture and Social Change: Selected Papers*. Chicago: University of Chicago Press.

Papajohn, J. and Speigel, J.P. (1975). *Transactions in Families: A Modern Approach to Resolving Cultural and Generational Conflict*. London: Jossey-Bass.

Ramakrishnan, K.R. and Balgopal, P.R. (1985-86). Task-Centered Casework: Intervention Strategy for Developing Societies. *Journal of International and Comparative Social Welfare*. 2:21-28.

Spiegel, J. (1982). An Ecological Model of Ethnic Families. In *Ethnicity and Family Therapy*. M. McGoldrick, J. Pearce, and J. Giordano (Eds.). London: Guilford.

Varma, B.N. (1980). Indians as New Ethnics: A Theoretical Note. In *The New Ethnics*. P. Saran and E. Eames (Eds.). New York: Praeger.

Vignehsa, H. and Minai, K. (1988). Socialisation and the Singapore Family: The nature of Socialisation Values, Principles of Socialisation and Structural Parameters. *Abstract* (mimeographed). National University of Singapore, 7 September.

Yutang, L. (Ed.) (1942). *The Wisdom of India and China*. New York: Random House.

Zimmer, H. (1951)., *Philosophies of India*. New York: Bollingen Foundation.

# Application of Single-Session Groups in Working with Vietnamese Refugees in Hong Kong

Lik-man Chan

**SUMMARY.** With the gradual implementation of the liberalization policy which gave the refugees in closed centres more chances to move about in the community and to take up open employment, social agencies serving these camps launched new programs to meet their rising needs. The Work Orientation Program (the Program) described in this paper is an exigent measure to help the growing number of refugees from this centre with jobs to adjust to their new work environment and to the Hong Kong society at large. As single session groups are the main tools used in the Program, this paper, apart from describing the contents and effectiveness of the Program, also discusses the application of this group work mode in working with this special ethnic group and the related implications.

The massive exodus of Vietnamese refugees since 1975 has become a burden for Hong Kong and many other countries. During the fourteen years that Hong Kong has faced this problem, it has tried out a variety of different policies. Public opinion shifted frequently between sympathy and acceptance on the one hand to blame and rejection on the other. Despite such volatility, Hong Kong still has to face the reality of having to host the 25,000 Vietnamese refugees and asylum seekers in various open and closed centres (UNHCR/A, Hollmann, 1989). To serve these unexpected arrivals,

Lik-man Chan, MA, is Lecturer, Department of Social Work, The Chinese University of Hong Kong, Shatin, N.T., Hong Kong.

The author wishes to thank the staff members of Caritas—Hong Kong, particularly Mrs. Teresa Lam and Miss Sylvia Leung for their help and support in providing the relevant information for this paper.

*103*

voluntary agencies have been making tremendous contributions parallel to the efforts put forth by the Hong Kong Government and the United Nations High Commissioner for Refugees (UNHCR). Caritas—Hong Kong, for example, has launched a Work Orientation Program (the Program) to help refugees in a liberalizing closed centre with job offers to adjust to their future work and a special group work approach was employed in delivering the service. This paper presents a general account on the Vietnamese refugees' situation in Hong Kong and discusses the use of single-session groups as an approach to help this refugee group adapt and integrate into Hong Kong.

## VIETNAMESE REFUGEES IN HONG KONG

When the Vietnamese began their exodus in 1975, they were received by the people of Hong Kong with a surge of pity underpinned by humanitarian spirits. They were then placed in open camps with freedom to move about in the community and to seek work outside the camp. The ultimate hope of the refugees was to resettle in a developed country and the United States was the dreamt country for most of them (Editorial, *Welfare Digest*, 1979). Through these years, Canada, Austria and the U.S.A. continue to be the main resettlement countries for these refugees but the rate of resettlement has been falling from 3,746 in 1980 to 2,772 in 1988 (Refugee Division, Security Branch, Hong King, 1989a). The reason for this slow down in resettlement rate was economic and high unemployment in the receiving countries. These countries also began to get tired of the strain of resettlement (Editorial, *Welfare Digest*, 1983). Davis (1988) also noted that funding for the resettlement program was drying up and resettlement countries began to close their doors. This meant that the refugees would remain in Hong Kong for an indefinite length of time. Furthermore, the situation was aggravated by the continued influx of refugees every year (Refugee Division, Security Branch, Hong Kong, 1989a), creating great economic burden and management problem for Hong Kong. In July 1987, the Hong Kong Government introduced the closed camp measure as a means to enforce its policy of humane deterrence; i.e., new arrivals after that said date would be placed in a closed camp indefinitely awaiting their resettlement. However, this measure did not achieve the expected deterrent effect on the Vietnamese as evidenced by the great number of new arrivals in the subsequent years (Refugee Division, Security Branch, Hong Kong, 1989a). This led to Hong Kong Government's adopting a screening policy on June 16, 1988 through which boat people from Vietnam were screened to be classified either as "political refugees," "economic migrants," or "illegal immigrants." According to international agreement, only "political refugees" would enjoy the right of not being repatriated to the country of origin, and the place of first asylum had the obligation to make arrangements for their resettlement. On the other hand, "illegal immigrants" do not have such rights and would face repatriation. Hence, the Hong Kong Government is seeking internationally acceptable arrangements for repatriation for those boat people not classified as genuine refugees. Although the screening policy was another measure to stem the influx of Vietnamese refugees, its effectiveness was pitilessly challenged by the arrival of nine thousand newcomers within the half year after the screening policy was enforced (Refugees Division, Security Branch, Hong Kong, 1989c). It seems that more international efforts are needed before the Vietnamese refugees' problem could be settled.

Under the closed camp policy, the majority of the Vietnamese refugees was accommodated in the closed centres. As a policy, the closed camp concept had been received as a regrettable but understandable measure (Editorial, *Welfare Digest*, 1983). However, the conditions in the closed camps were being strongly criticised. McPherson (1983) pointed out that the refugees in closed camps have no basic freedom. Fozzard (1985) commented that "the Vietnamese refugees in Closed Camps were suspended physically, socially, emotionally and intellectually in a kind of 'no man's land' between the familiar past and the unknown future. . . . The Closed Centre is in every way a total Institution" (P. 3). Davis (1988) expressed strong concern over the huge number of children "imprisoned in the centres as they would be deprived from growing up with primary experiences and educational and development opportunities essential for a physically and healthy upbringing." Strong protests were made to open up the closed centers. Yau (1988) believed that, by so doing, it would be beneficial both to the mental health of the refugees as well as their chance of emigration. Bale (1988) argued that allowing refugees to live openly in the community would save money, would ease staffing pressure on the responsible government department, would help the serious labour shortage and would allow the refugees to live a more normal life.

In response to the humanitarian concerns and following an agreement made with UNHCR on the screening policy in 1988, the Hong Kong Government undertook to 'liberalize' conditions in closed camps for Vietnamese refugees who had arrived before the screening policy in June, 1988. As the 'liberalization' measures were being implemented, Kumin (1989b), noted that refugee life in the closed centres was gradually changed, restrictions on freedom of movement were progressively lifted and "children were to be allowed out of the camps for education, adults for vocational training and employment, and in general people were to be allowed to go out for recreation and social activities" (Kumin, 1989b, p. 24).

## CULTURAL ORIENTATION

The gradual liberalization of the closed centres has brought the Vietnamese refugees in Hong Kong more opportunities to move about freely in the Hong Kong community before their resettlement to other countries. Unfortunately, the slowing down of the resettlement process has lengthened the period of the refugees' temporary stay in Hong Kong. There are worries that finally Hong Kong would have to keep all those refugees who are unable to resettle to other countries (Editorial, *Welfare Digest*, 1983, p. 2; Yau, 1988, p. 3). Suggestions have been made to find "a more comprehensive plan which will prepare this potential residue of 'difficult to place' group for full integration" (Editorial, *Welfare Digest*, 1983, p. 2). Social service agencies are implementing different programs to meet emerging needs of this group of refugees, demonstrating the spirit of the Geneva Conference (1979) in their concern about people, not politics and their interest in placing an immediate humanitarian response, not guilt to the tragic Vietnamese refugees' problem (Stumpf, 1979). Social service agencies providing services in closed centres immediately started planning programs to help the refugees adjust to the Hong Kong society. Caritas—Hong Kong, for example, launched a Cultural Orientation Project starting from October, 1988 in the Shamshuipo Closed Centre. The aims of the project were to "to better prepare themselves (the refugees) to function as dignified human persons, to cope for overseas settlement and to better adjust to the local community life after the liberalization of the camps" (Caritas—Hong Kong, 1989). The second obvious goal was to provide Vietnamese refugees access to sufficient resources to allow them to maintain their ethnic identity within Chinese Hong Kong. The Cultural Orientation Project was conducted through mass programs and small groups. Given through mass programs was information on (1) the laws of Hong Kong, i.e., labour laws, criminal laws and civil laws; (2) legal rights; (3) personal hygiene and medical service; (4) banking service, and (5) the education and communication systems. Topics delivered through small groups which allowed the use of role plays and discussions were:

1. geography and human living
2. community life, various types of social service and facilities, e.g., postal and police service, art center activities
3. transportation, e.g., different types, passenger classes; bus routes; road safety
4. shopping and money
5. social atmosphere, e.g., the general feeling and attitudes of Hong Kong people towards Vietnamese refugees
6. customs, taboos, major festivals and some simple Cantonese (the major dialect used by Chinese in Hong Kong)
7. sex roles/parenting—the importance of protection of women and children and clarification of the views about women's status, wife battering and child abuse in Hong Kong.

Working across cultures denotes the co-existence of differing life styles and social norms, and they should be encouraged or allowed (Cheetham, 1982). The above program content is important for acquainting the Vietnamese refugees with the social norms held in Hong Kong. They should facilitate the socio-cultural adjustment of the Vietnamese refugees whose permanent stay in Hong Kong is mostly unintended and uncertain. Eventually, it is hoped that by attending to the unique conditions of the refugees and acquainting them to the cultural conditions of Hong Kong, the refugees could become more bicultural and more successful in their adaptation to employment and life in a new cultural environment such as Hong Kong.

## WORK ORIENTATION PROGRAM

The mental health state and employment opportunities of the refugees are two of the major areas that have received increased concern (Roberts et al. 1982; Land et al. 1988; Nishimoto, 1988). With the enforcement of the liberalization policy, Vietnamese refugees in closed centres are given access to open employment. Actually, to be able to work had been the wish of many refugees (Tu, 1985). In their 1982 study on the mental health status of Indochinese refugees in Hong Kong, Roberts, Chau, Nishimoto and Mok had already urged that "camp life should be structured to facilitate meaningful employment and to provide social interaction" (p. 47). They also found that meaningful employment while in camp enhanced the refuges' abilities to cope with the stresses of refugee life (p. 46). This was further echoed by a voluntary agency worker that "employment is the fastest possible way for these people (Vietnamese refugees) to regain their sense of dignity and self-reliance" (Kumin, 1989c, p. 26). Besides, the provision of interim employment opportunities is regarded as a preventive service to the refugees (Land, Nishimoto & Chau, 1988). Recently, the refugees' desire to work was realized by the many employment opportunities made available by eager employers who sought out suitable refugees from the camps. Such opportunities were made possible by the economic boom and the labour shortage in Hong Kong. There was a good number of openings in fast food service, garment factories and supermarkets.

Recent statistics revealed that over 2000 refugees from the liberalized camps had obtained employment (Kumin, 1989b) creating a concomitant need for the refugees to adjust to the work environment. The Work Orientation Program (the Program) implemented by Caritas was designed as an exigent measure to help refugees from the Shamshuipo Camp take up employment. The urgency of the Program was evident by having to serve a great number of refugees (ranging from 10 to 100) at one time, normally within two weeks' time. The Program formed a very important part of the Cultural Orientation Project, and is aimed at helping the refugees to achieve cultural, economic and social adjustment to Hong Kong.

The Program functions to lower the participants' anxiety toward a strange environment and toward tasks related to their new job by providing them with basic information as well as emotional and social support.

The contents of the Program consisted of the following items, most of which were practical in nature:

1. *The use of "Flashcards"*

   Explanation on the purpose, contents and the using of the "Flashcard" distributed to each participant. The "Flashcard" was of business card size containing eight short questions written in Chinese and in Vietnamese to facilitate the refugees to make enquiries under special circumstances, e.g., get lost. An example of the question is "Please tell me how to go to the nearest police station."

2. *From camp to place of work*

   This included explanation on the procedures of leaving the camp; map reading; the specific route and mode of transportation to their working place.

3. *Using public transport*

   Points had to be noted when using public transport such as bus, Mass Transit Railway (MTR). Examples are:

   A. Line up at the bus stop.
   B. Enter the bus at the front door and pay the exact fare on entry.
   C. Observe rules on the bus, e.g., no smoking on the lower deck.
   D. Using the MTR ticket machine.
   E. The procedures of passing through the MTR "entry gate" and "exit gate."
   F. No smoking inside the MTR car.

4. *Work attitudes and general behaviour*

   A. Not to be late for work or to leave early.
   B. Work hard and no sleeping or taking a nap during work.

C. Do not take anything from the working place back to the centre.
D. Not to chit-chat too much at work or shout across the room.
E. Not to fight with other workers.
F. Inform the employer of sick leave/annual leave. Permission for these leaves must be sought before and not afterwards.

Some advice on general behavior included:

A. Not to fight. It is illegal to fight in the street.
B. Not to litter or spit.
C. Not to 'squat' in the street which was their habit in Vietnam.
D. Men not to hold hands or to tease girls. (It was very normal in their culture for males to hold hands.)
E. Pay attention to the male/female toilet signs.
F. Be cooperative with the police and not to run, quarrel or hit the police when being requested to present their identity.

5. *Important camp rules*
Reminding the refugees not to bring forbidden items or anything in large quantity into the camp and to be punctual in returning to the camp.
6. *Using telephone*
Teaching the refugees how to use the telephone and to remember the telephone number of the camp.
7. *Money and currency*
Helping refugees to differentiate the various types of coins and paper note and to open a bank account if necessary.
8. *Eating outside the camp*
Familiarizing the refugees with the restaurants/food centres near their working place and the appropriate way of making payment. Instruction on some basic food names and eating habits/hygiene.
9. *Road safety*
Information on the basic traffic knowledge and rules plus the warning that failure to obey certain regulations may be prosecuted.

10. *Use of lift and escalators*
     Teaching the various types of switches inside the lift and points to note when using escalators.
11. *Shopping*
     Providing information on markets, supermarkets, department stores and some related rules. Giving the caution that there are hidden cameras and security guards in the stores and that taking away things without paying is a criminal offense that can affect one's application for resettlement in other countries.
12. *Basic labour rules/regulations*
     Information on the labour rules related to the Hong Kong situation.

## MODE OF SERVICE DELIVERY

The above contents were presented by means of two single-session groups, one for briefing, the other for outing and some supplementary services given between the group meetings.

*Briefing Session.* This was a one and one-half hour single session for all the refugees who had to take up employment within two weeks' time. The session was conducted in the form of a big group to cater to the great number of participants. Contents covered in this briefing session were general information for all participants covering items 1, 3, 4, 5, and 9 listed above. The session was conducted by a qualified social worker and a Camp Aid (a Vietnamese refugee and an employee of Caritas with the ability to speak English and Cantonese which is the primary Chinese dialect spoken in Hong Kong).

The following is an example of the time break-down of a typical briefing session:

A. Introduction on the agency,
   camp rules and
   the usage of the "Flashcard."                     15 minutes
B. Information on work ethics and
   the appropriate behaviour in
   work environment and in the community.            30 minutes

C. Information on transportation,
   (mainly about MTR and bus)
   and on road safety.                                    30 minutes
D. General information on the
   employing organizations and
   question time.                                         15 minutes

*Worksite Visit.* Following the briefing session, the participants
were taken to visit their respective worksites before they reported
for duty. Liaison work with the employers was done by the social
worker who arranged the date of the 'outing' and other details. Refugees with the same employer were grouped together and normally
there were 5-8 members in one group, with two or more than ten
groups attending the briefing session at one particular time.

Apart from providing participants the chance to see the working
place, the Worksite Visit also served as a practice session for the
whole Program, covering content items 2, 6, 8, 10, and 11 listed
above. The time needed for the Worksite Visit varied with different
groupings and it might range from one and one-half hours to six
hours, depending on the location of the worksites. Each Worksite
Visit group was led by a volunteer (mostly Westerners belonging to
a voluntary organization, Dutch Charity Fund) and a Camp Aid
who served as an interpreter. The normal sequence of a Worksite
Visit was:

A. Reaching the worksite and a brief orientation given by the employer. Discussions among the group members were encouraged.
B. Return to the Shamshuipo district (location of the Closed Centre) where the members will be given time to practise shopping
   in the neighborhood stores. Afterwards, the participants had to
   return to the closed centre.

*Supplementary Services.* In the interim between the Briefing Session and the Worksite Visit, individualized services such as assistance in opening a bank account and photo-taking for identity cards
would be provided. By going through such process, the refugees
were introduced to the banking service, money and currency in

Hong Kong (Item 7 of the Program contents listed above). Besides, there were talks on basic labour rules/regulations (Item 12) arranged for participants coming from several briefing groups within that particular period. Escort service or transportation to worksite on the first day of employment was arranged by the Hong Kong Christian Aid to Refugees, a voluntary agency, through liaison with the respective employers.

## RESPONSE AND EFFECTIVENESS

Evaluation is an important component of the Program. Volunteers who served in the Worksite Visit were requested to complete an evaluation on that session for the worker's reference in evaluating the Program. Views of the Camp Aids and the participants were also gathered. As the Program had been run for just a few months, an overall evaluation on its effectiveness had not been formally made. However, a very small scale informal survey of the participants' views on the effectiveness of the Program was done by the social worker in February, 1989. Feedbacks were gathered from 26 out of 450 participants in the Program. It was learnt that 19 of them continued with their employment while 7 had dropped out. They all found the Briefing Session useful and effective in helping them adjust to the work environment and life in Hong Kong. Two pieces of information they regarded to be of particular help were (1) the need to inform their boss before taking time off from work and (2) the warning on some inappropriate general behaviours, i.e., to squat in the street and to delay payment for commodities which they took away. All the 26 respondents found the Worksite Visit session effective and useful in (1) helping them to know the route to work, and (2) familiarizing them with the place of work through guided tour. They were all happy to have the chance to do some shopping on their way back. However, they suggested some areas for improvement, namely, (1) to provide them with more detailed information about their prospective employment, e.g., types of duty; (2) to inform them of the number of leave days, fringe benefits, salary structure related to their work, and (3) to discuss with them the chance of changing jobs.

Apparently, the effectiveness of the Program could be judged by the high percentage (73%) of participants still staying with their initial employment. These 19 participants had worked for their employers for more than three months and they all found no problem in adjusting to their work. They further pointed out that their understanding of some basic Cantonese had been helpful. For the 7 (27%) participants who dropped out from their work, five quit their jobs in fast food service because the jobs involved a lot of hard work and long work hours, but no salary increase. One left the factory job finding the employer stingy and exploitative. Another participant was fired because of absence from work.

Speaking overall, all the participants found the total Program useful. They felt that the information on labour laws and on their legal rights (especially when being questioned by police) had been particularly useful for providing them with the knowledge to protect themselves.

## THE GROUP WORK APPROACH

The Vietnamese refugees joining the local work force create a unique group presenting special needs that warrant a unique service program. The Work Orientation Program and its mode of delivery constitute that unique Program. As mentioned, single-session groups were the major tools used in the Program. Single-session groups, variously referred to as single-meeting groups (Schwartz, 1971), one session meetings (Shalinsky, 1983), and single session collectivities (Clarke, 1986), are receiving increasing attention in group work literature (Middleman and Goldberg, 1987). Although there was debate as to whether a single-session group is an aggregate or a group (Shalinsky, 1983), single-session groups are regarded as one of the variant elements in group practice (Shulman, 1979), even though they fail to meet the criteria of the mainstream group described by Papell and Rothman in many aspects. For example, the worker in a single-session group has difficulties in meeting the essential demand 'to further linkages between members as they engage in active participation in group building while striving to meet their own needs' (Papell and Rothman, 1980a, p. 12). According to Casper (1983), however, a single-session group is a group because it fits Casper's definition of 'two or more persons in interaction around a commonality of time however brief' (Quoted in Alissi and Casper, 1985). It has gained the status of being a classical example of the short-term, time-limited group (Alissi and Casper, 1985). In fact, single-session groups do have their part to play in serving a big number of people with similar needs to be met with urgency. Shulman further points out that single session groups can be quite effective if properly and skillfully structured (1979, p. 266).

In the Work Orientation Program, two separate but related single-session groups (one for briefing and the other for worksite visit) were used. This special approach worked extremely well in serving the great number of refugees requiring special help within a period of two weeks. For such a big client group, serving the members individually was time-consuming and impractical. Furthermore, if the casework method was used, it would deprive the service recipients of peer influence and support that a single-session group could provide. On the other hand, the use of small groups with more frequent meetings was also not feasible due to limitation of time. Hence, the service mode adopted by the Program seemed to be the most appropriate one. Basically, the Program had made tactful application of single-session groups. Although each single session group had its particular function (briefing or worksite visit) to perform, it was the differential use of them supplemented by additional services between sessions that had helped to achieve the aims of the entire Program. The different size of the two single session groups was a necessary and appropriate design. It was practical for the briefing session to include a greater number of participants for convenience of information presentation, while the small size of the Worksite Visit groups functioned to promote mutual sharing and interactions among the members. This design fit in well with the two approaches to one-session meetings described by Shalinsky (1983), i.e., one attempted to encourage some sense of group and some form of interaction among the members and the other focused on a lecture/public meeting format (Shalinsky, 1983, p. 915). It is obvious that both these formats were applied in the Program.

Having to complete the necessary services to the refugees within two weeks, the Program definitely faced time constraint. However, time constraint did not constitute any disadvantage to the Program owing to a great extent to its use of single-session group formats. Block (1985) points out that single session groups help to destroy the illusion of unending time and Hartford (1971) holds that the knowledge of time limited duration may encourage a group to work and to complete the objectives as soon as possible. All these serve to remind the workers in single session groups to be time-focused. In fact, the workers in the Program had made very conscious use of the time available. Proper mastery of time was seen from the careful allotment of time in the Briefing Session in which information and materials were given in a concise and clear way. The sequencing of the Worksite Visits also helped much in achieving the goals set.

The group work approach used by the Program did not find its exact affiliation to any particular model or theory presented in group work literature (Papell and Rothman, 1980b, Roberts and Northen, 1976). It could be regarded as a special mode on its own, whose potential to become a new approach to the practice of social work with groups invites additional work. Furthermore, the initial, positive results of the Program had suggested the workability of such an approach and demonstrated that the unique needs in the refugee populations did require a special form of service delivery.

One thing worthy of special note is the contribution of the Camp Aids who served as interpreters in the Program and had thus facilitated all communication processes in the service delivery. Their service in the group sessions as well as in providing supplementary services was essential. The use of bilingual staff has been considered important in providing service to client groups of a different ethnic origin (British Association of Social Workers, 1978, Editorial; Jenkins, 1981).

## IMPLICATIONS

The Program by providing skills for the Vietnamese refugees to maintain their employment also provides bridges for them to adapt to the new Hong Kong culture. The independence provided by employment allows for the maintenance of the Vietnamese culture within the dominant Chinese society. Moreover, implicit attention to problems of cultural preservation during the single-session groups will be made more explicit during additional follow-up sessions with Program participants after they have been working for some months.

From the above discussions, there are several implications for the Program itself for further application of the single-session group approach, and how they enhance ethnicity and cultural adaptation.

(1) Despite the effectiveness achieved, the Program should consider the suggestions made by the service consumers in the informal survey described above for further improvement. To maintain the services of the volunteers and the Camp Aids in the Program is necessary.

(2) The Program participants attending the same Briefing and Worksite Visit sessions can be helped to develop into more permanent groups. In fact, Shalinsky (1983) has pointed out that single-session meetings do stand a chance of proceeding from an aggregate to a group if given additional help (p. 924). The Program participants possess good potential for such a move because of the following reasons:

A. They belong to the same ethnic group with similar background and cultural practice and are facing the same situation.
B. They live in the same centre and may be easier to recruit for meetings.
C. They have already had a chance to meet in the Briefing Session and to interact in the Worksite Visit.
D. Some of them are working for the same employer and in the same locality.

Program activities for such groups can focus on sharing and discussions of difficulties encountered in work, as well as conflicts or incongruence arising out of cultural differences. It is also helpful to arrange joint meetings with local groups and to involve more local Chinese residents to help in running the groups' program activities. Through such actions, the Program participants can be further helped to adjust to the culture of Hong Kong. Besides, mutual support spirits among the members can be nurtured and the groups can even be helped to achieve a more autonomous form similar to that stated in Lang's formulation (1972).

(3) The group work approach adopted by the Program can be applied to the other program items in the Cultural Orientation Project to be launched in the liberalizing closed centres. Modified applications of the single-session groups can be contemplated.

(4) Single-Session groups can be used to serve various types of client systems, for example, foster parents (Shulman, 1979), patients (Shalinsky, 1983; Block, 1985); military families (Waldron et al. 1985), and families of spina bifida children (Clarke, 1986). It may also be possible to make use of such a group approach to help old people awaiting admission to aged homes and other ethnic groups in their initial stage of resettlement in a new cultural setting.

## *CONCLUSION*

The use of the group approach in helping minority ethnic groups as a possible means for facilitating cultural adaptation has been demonstrated by the Work Orientation Program for Vietnamese refugees. Single-session groups, the major tools used in the Program, proved to be helpful to introduce the refugees to their new work situation and to the novel cultural practices of Hong Kong. With additional opportunities, these single-session groups will be used to maintain a multicultural environment in Chinese Hong Kong.

## REFERENCES

Alissi, A.S.; Casper, M. (1985). Time as a factor in social groupwork. *Social Work With Groups*. *8*(2), 3-16.

Bale, C. (1988). Refugee policy must be humanitarian. *Welfare Digest*, *171*, 4.

Block, L.R. (1985). On the potentiality and limits of time: the single-session group and the cancer patient. *Social Work With Groups*. *8*(2), 81-99.

British Association of Social Workers (1978). *Studies in inter-cultural social work*. Birmingham: British Association of Social Workers.

Caritas — Hong Kong (1989). *Diary, January, 1989*. Hong Kong: Caritas — Hong Kong.

Clarke, E.(1986). The use of single session collectivities with families of spina bifida children. *Social Work With Groups*. *9*(4), 103-111.

Cheetham, J. (Ed.) (1982). *Social work and ethnicity*. London: George Allen & Unwin.

Davis, L. (1988). Hong Kong and the Indochinese refugees. *Welfare Digest*, *171*, 1-2.

Fozzard, S. (1985). Closed camps—"no man's land." *Welfare Digest, 134,* 3.

Hartford, M.E. (1971). *Groups in social work.* New York: Columbia University Press.

Hong Kong Council of Social Service, (1979). *Welfare Digest,* Issue No. 64.

Hong Kong Council of Social Service, (1983). *Welfare Digest,* Issue No. 110.

Hong Kong Council of Social Service, (1985). *Welfare Digest,* Issue No. 134.

Hong Kong Council of Social Service, (1988). *Welfare Digest,* Issue No. 171.

Jenkins, S. (1981). *The ethnic dilemma in social services.* New York: The Free Press.

Kumin, J. (1989a). Is the boat full? *Refugees, 61,* 20-23.

Kumin, J. (1989b). Government explains new refugee policy. *Refugees. 61,* 23-25.

Kumin, J. (1989c). Opening the doors. *Refugees, 61,* 25-26.

Land, H., Nishimoto, R. & Chau, K. (1988). Interventive and preventive services for Vietnamese Chinese refugees. *Social Service Review.* 62(3), 468-484.

Lang, N.C. (1972). A broad-range model of practice in the social work group. *Social Service Review.* 46(1), 76-89.

McPherson, J. (1983). Closed camps for Vietnamese refugees in Hong Kong. *Welfare Digest, 110,* 3.

Middleman, R.R., & Goldberg, G. (1987). Social work practice with groups. In A. Minehan et al. (Eds.) *Encyclopedia of social work,* (18th ed. pp. 714-729). Silver Spring, Maryland: National Association of Social Workers.

Nishimoto, R. (1988). A cross-cultural analysis of psychiatric symptom expression using Langer's twenty-two item index. *Journal of Sociology & Social Work.* 15(4), 45-62.

Papell, C., & Rothman, B. (1980a). Relating the mainstream model of social work with groups to group psychotherapy and the structured group approach. *Social Work With Groups.* 3(2), 5-23.

Papell, C., & Rothman, B. (1980b). Social group work models: possession and heritage. In A.S. Alissi (Ed.), *Perspectives on social group work practice, a book of readings* (pp. 116-132). New York: The Free Press.

Refugees Division, Security Branch, Hong Kong (February, 1989a). *Fact sheet, Vietnamese boat people in Hong Kong.*

Refugees Division, Security Branch, Government Secretariat, Hong Kong, (February, 1989b). *Executive summary.*

Refugees Division, Security Branch, Government Secretariat, Hong Kong, (February, 1989c). *Monthly statistical report (Arrivals and departures).*

Refugees Division, Security Branch, Government Secretariat, Hong Kong, (February, 1989d). *Vietnamese boat people in Hong King: what the Hong Kong government has done.*

Roberts, R. W., Chau, K.L., Nishimoto, R.H. & Mok, B. (1982). Refugees at risk: some covariates of mental health status. *The Hong Kong Journal of Social Work,* 16(1/2), 38-47.

Roberts, R. & Northen, H. (Eds.) (1976). *Theories of social work with groups.* New York: Columbia University Press.

Schwartz, W. (1971). On the use of groups in social work practice. In W. Schwartz & S.R. Zalba (Eds.) *The practice of group work* (pp. 3-24). New York: Columbia University Press.

Shalinsky, W. (1983). One session meetings: aggregate or group? In N. Goroff (Ed.). *Reaping from the field—from practice to principle*. Hebron, Connecticut: Practitioners Press, 896-929.

Shulman, L. (1979). *The Skills of helping individuals and groups*. Itasca, Illinois: F.E.Peacock Publishers, Inc.

Stumpf, K.L. (1979). In search of a global solution. *Welfare Digest, 134*, 4.

Tu, E.E. (1985). Closed camps for Vietnamese refugees. *Welfare Digest, 134*, 4.

United Nations High Commissioner for Refugees, (January, 1989). *Information paper*. Geneva: United Nations High Commissioner for Refugees.

UNHCR/A. Hollmann (1989). Waiting for an answer. *Refugees, 61*, 19.

Waldron, J.A., Whittington, R.R. & Jensen, S. (1985). Children's single-session briefings: group work with military families experiencing parents' deployment. *Social Work With Groups. 8*(2), 101-109.

Yau, S. (1988). The boat people problem. *Welfare Digest, 171*, 2-3.

# A GAMING OPPORTUNITY
# FOR MULTI-ETHNIC
# GROUP EXPERIENCE

These three short pieces offer an opportunity for participants to experience selected dynamics of being members of ethnic minority or other "risk" groups, develop ethnic sensitivity and culture self-awareness, and to enhance skills for intercultural understanding.

# The Basic Game

Paul Abels
Sonia Leib Abels

## *INTRODUCTION*

The teacher often needs to create a setting in which systems reflecting social class, cross-cultural concerns, disrespectful treatment of ethnic groups, abuse of power and the frustrations of seeking help in unfriendly circumstances can be explored, understood, and "felt." This is often the case in classes which do not reflect ethnic diversity or experiences with a wide spectrum of social groups.

We present here a flexible teaching/learning simulation which permits adaptation to a broad range of content in various settings. This gaming approach is particularly suitable in teaching the systems perspective. It provides an opportunity to set up a social class and/or hierarchical structure in which "clients," "risk groups," etc., have to negotiate with intermediaries in order to reach their goals. The power structure can be supportive or oppressive. The workers advocates or reticent. Conflicts may arise unexpectedly and need to be considered.

*The format*: The instructor must be clear as to the analytical framework (topic) to be explored and reflected upon as it determines the simulation assignment. The simulation occurs within a context: community, agency, corporation, planning group, ethics committee, grant review board, family, bureau, etc. Every situation allows examination of the analytical perspective and dynamics of

Paul Abels, PhD, is Professor of Social Work, California State University, Long Beach, CA. Sonia Leib Abels, MSW, is Consultant, Trainer, University of California, Davis, Extension Programs.

*123*

the social unit (family, group, community, etc.), and can be so structured as to reflect ethnic and cultural diversity.

Groups of 4-10 persons are formed. Assignment of persons to groups may be random or according to a design. (The instructor assigns roles, or places people together for particular educational reasons.) The game is usually played with three groups but can be expanded.

*Materials:* Poker chips and a list of the value of each color chip. Drawing materials (chalk board, newsprint or notebook paper, markers). More elaborate materials can be selected for the purpose of enhancing the game.

*Time:* The simulation can be completed within a class meeting or carried over. The ideal time is about two hours, including debriefing. An hour and fifteen minutes for the game and about another 45 minutes for reflecting and debriefing. However the time limit can be set relative to the progression of the simulation. That is, the instructor might want to halt or continue the game as s/he evaluates the movement within the simulation.

## INSTRUCTIONS

1. Assign all groups a task related to the selected topic, i.e., "In two minutes define power, system, boundaries, small group, culture", etc.

2. Award chips to the group with the best results and to the group that finished first. The decision can be made by the instructor or by a judge. The instructor awards the chips.

3. Assign more difficult tasks, i.e., "In three minutes be prepared to explain to the class the differences between group work and group therapy. Develop a demonstration to illustrate systems at work, a community conflict, or a family problem, and present it to the class." *Award chips to the best presentation*.

4. During the above described processes, seek opportunities to reward a deviant. If a judge selects a "best presentation" and the first to finish, award chips to the group that finishes last, or to the

person that asks a question, or objects, etc. You are helping create ambiguity.

5. Give the group one less chip then there are members and ask them to distribute the chips to their group.

## VARIABLES

The following instructions add complexity and conflict to the simulation and can be used flexibly. They need to be specifically related to the desired outcomes.

6. You may give one or more task, and reward similarly.

7. Have each group add up their chips according to their worth and make the results public. A hierarchy is established among the groups based on their totals.

    a. Those with the most chips have the greatest autonomy and power. They are the establishment, the corporation, the executive director, the manager, city council, wealthy developer, gang, board, non-ethnic, etc.

    b. A second group are social workers, supervisors, community agents, teachers, middle class families, etc.

    c. The group with the least amount of chips are clients, aides, the poor, the most vulnerable, women, ethnic minorities, the aged, etc.

8. Tasks are assigned each group.

    a. The most vulnerable group, the one with the least chips, are assigned the task of putting together a "request." This may be in the form of a petition, a plan, a funding proposal or some other need to be met. This is to be presented to the high ranking group, "the establishment."

        This group usually reflects the vulnerable groups in society, the poor, ethnic minorities, women, etc.

    b. The most powerful group, the high ranking group makes up the remaining rules for the game. The other group must follow instructions, the powerless group can only speak through the "helpers," the middle group. The instructor, however can always modify the rules, and can always reward chips and take some away capriciously.

c. The power group can give extra chips to the poor, who if they accumulate enough chips can replace the workers in the middle group, and the middle group drops down to the poverty level, etc., etc.

9. The game can end in a number of ways. The power group can grant the request, a decision to end can be made by the instructor, at times the "client" group refuses to continue.

## REFLECTIONS

Following the game we have been able to discuss with the class the idea of open communication, power, control, systems, cybernetics, how decisions get made, what happens in a stalemate, the poor refusing to play the game, feelings about deviants, unfair rewards, punishment, etc. How did they decide to distribute chips to each other when there was one less chip than members? If the game is played with agency staff, observations of interrelations, stress communication patterns may serve as clues to agency needs, change and ideas for future training programs.

## CAUTION

This game can bring out some strong feelings related to "just treatments" by you and/or the power group. It is important to have the groups discuss their feelings about the experience in addition to their learnings. Be alert to rising feelings and end the game at an appropriate point.

The game can be modified in a number of ways. If the learning task is related to ethnic and cultural differences, then the three group tasks can be more complex, requiring more time and instruction. If the learning is related to conflict resolution or intergroup communication, the game can be structured to allow more opportunities for interaction among the groups, and/or among group members.

# Teaching Ethno-Racial Sensitivity Through Groups

Urania Glassman

## INTRODUCTION

This outline describes the use of small group role plays which replicate an actual program to teach the development of ethno-racial sensitivity through small groups. These role plays have been used in foundation practice classes in the first year master's curriculum. The specific learning tasks addressed include (a) appreciating the value of small groups of people representing a diversity of ethnic and racial groups as a way to combat ethnocentrism and bias; (b) recognizing the importance of developing interactional programs to address the highly emotionally charged area of racial and ethnic relations; and (c) recognizing the important role social workers can play in organizing key community groups for prevention and planning in the area of interracial understanding.

## GROUP WORK PROGRAM TO COMBAT PREJUDICE

The work of the Montgomery County Human Relations Commission in Bethesda, Maryland (Weiss and Ephross, 1986), which uses varied group work approaches with perpetrators of hate, violence, victims, and community groups is exemplary. In cooperation with the courts, teenagers who have committed crimes of hate/violence, and their families may be placed into groups as a form of alternative service. Groups are used in an effort to educate and counsel people

---

Urania Glassman, MSW, is Assistant Professor, Direct Practice Faculty, Adelphi University, School of Social Work, Garden City, NY 11530.

*127*

who might have committed acts against persons of a different racial
or ethnic group.

For the victim, a cross burning, a swastika painted on a door, or
other harassments, bring up a history of prejudice that places the
person at risk of isolation and alienation in their home community
(Weiss and Ephross, 1986). Such a risk cannot afford to fester in
our communities. Victims' groups are organized to deal with the
incident and to re-establish trust and linkages to others in the community who are ethnically and racially not like them.

The community councils and coalitions were groups developed to
react to incidents of social disease. Not only did these affiliated
church, synagogue, school, police and political groups require the
necessary structures to respond to a crises in a rational and proactive
way, they also had to develop preventive actions and programs
within the community.

It was from knowledge of these efforts drawn from the papers
presented at the Group Work Symposium by Joan Weiss and Paul
Ephross that the role plays are derived.

## ROLE PLAYS

Three role plays replicating the Montgomery County program
were designed for the second semester practice class. They were to
be played consecutively in the class, with each group having a student worker-player as well.

The first group of victims consisted of a Jewish couple who had
swastikas painted on their door. The wife is the daughter of concen-
tration camp survivors. Both do not want to tell their children who
are away at college about the incident. Another character is a Puerto
Rican teacher who had graffiti painted all over his car about dating a
white woman. He knows it's kids from his school and wants to talk
about it in his classes. His girlfriend doesn't want to even come to
the group because she is so upset; she wants to move to a bigger city
because she feels they would have more anonymity. Another is a
Black pharmacist (Northern) and his wife who had a cross burned
on their lawn. The husband is not accustomed to this direct hatred,
while his wife expects it due to her childhood experiences in the
South. With them is the white drugstore owner who specifically

brought this man, from Howard University, to this town to eventually become his partner. The customers really like him, and he is here to support his friend and colleague. In addition, he feels the attack is also aimed at his business — they might as well have burned the cross on his lawn too, and he wants them to know that he will not be intimidated by this hatred.

The second group was the perpetrator-family group. The characters included a black teen who had painted a swastika on the door of a Jewish home, a white teen (German-Irish) who had harassed an inter-racial couple with obscene phone calls, a Jewish teen who had bothered 2 black deli store owners and one parent each. One parent was angry at her child, one was denying and one was sheepishly neutral.

The third group consists of the regional head of the National Council of Christians and Jews; the NAACP director; the Police Chief, the School Superintendent, the Anti-Defamation League representative, and a vocal local Black church leader. The worker is the chair of the County Human Rights Commission. At this meeting they had to deal with the aftermath of the Howard Beach incident (or verdicts) in their community.

The roles are written for each player, and distributed in the class, which is asked to break down into 3 groups. (Enough roles should be prepared for each class member.)

The first role play to begin is the group of victims. The instructor lets it run for about 10 minutes. Brief reaction time is permitted for discussion. The perpetrators role play is enacted, also for 10 minutes with a brief discussion period following. At the start of this role play, the student worker is given special support and affirmation, letting him or her know that the real workers find these groups very difficult to do. Finally, the community group is played and a brief discussion ensues. The importance of having the community group conducted by an influential community person is discussed. The central issues to be dealt with are discussed, and the varied worker approaches to and feelings about each group are considered. Relevant group work practice theory is discussed (Glassman and Kates, 1986a, 1986b, 1990; Glassman and Skolnik, 1984).

After discussion of each role play, the class is then reconstituted as a class. Bias murders at Howard Beach, and Bensonhurst are discussed as well as campus related issues. Participants now have a chance to talk about the effects of this kind of program and to examine the potential of developing similar programs in their own community, in the schools, and or through the agencies in which they are placed. It is most impactful for the class to know that this program is in fact a real one that has been in operation for several years.

Through these role plays and discussions students tune in to how helpful it is for victims of hate/violence to participate in cross-cultural groups. These foster empathy across interethnic lines. For perpetrators, the chance to be in cross-cultural groups helps prevent further ethnocentrism and prejudice. Students learn that program development and organization of the significant cultural groups in the community can be vital in fostering understanding and preventing bias incidents.

## REFERENCES

Glassman, Urania and Kates, Len. "The Use of Simulation Role Play to Teach Social Work Practice with Groups." Paper presented Council on Social Work Education, APM, Detroit, March, 1984.

Glassman, Urania and Kates, Len. "Techniques of Social Group Work," *Social Work with Groups*, Vol. 9: 1 Spring 1986a.

Glassman, Urania and Kates, Len. "Developing the Democratic Humanistic Norms of the Social Work Group," in Marvin Parnes (Ed.) *Innovations in Social Group Work*. N.Y.: Haworth Press, 1986b.

Glassman, Urania and Kates, Len. "Group Work: A Humanistic Approach." Newbury Park CA: Sage Publications, 1990.

Glassman, Urania and Skolnik, Louise. "The Role of Group Work in Refugee Resettlement," *Social Work with Groups* Vol. 7:1, Spring 1984.

Weiss, Joan and Ephross, Paul, "Group Work Approaches to Hate/Violence Incidents. Paper presented at the Fifth Annual Symposium on Social Work with Groups, Detroit, October 1986. Printed in Social Work, Vol. 31:2, March/April 1986, Rockville, MD.

# What's New?

## Ruthann L. Rountree

There are three goals for this game: (1) provide the participants with an experience of social systems; (2) set up a mock social system that demonstrates differential privilege and opportunity based upon status; and (3) introduce a change agent who will represent an alternative chance to win the game.

## *PROCESS*

The game is played in two phases. In Phase I, all participants are given a brief introduction: "We are going to play a game that simulates some of the problems faced by racial or ethnic group members. The name of the game is 'What's New?'. The object of the game is to fill the 'position sheet' with status badges. The first three people to fill their 'position sheets' win."

### Instructions (Phase I)

Based upon the length of your name you will receive status badges. You are to wear the 'position sheets' pinned on your shirt/ blouse. There are two tables with sheets of badges and scissors (participants do not know one is dull). You may cut one and then return to the end of either line. Persons with more badges may cut in line of those with fewer badges.

Ruthann L. Rountree, MSW, MDiv, is affiliated with California State University, Long Beach, Department of Social Work, 1250 Bellflower Blvd., Long Beach, CA 90840-0902.

### Instructions (Phase II)

When some of the participants had at least half of their sheets full, a CHANGE AGENT is brought on the scene. This agent is selected from the group and given the instructions: "You represent a *new system* of social reform that is going to introduce to the community a better way of improving one's social position. You will have a quantity of pre-cut badges of contrasting color. Your object is to get people to use your supply. Make up any advertising approach you want, the only catch is that the backs of the blue badges are marked with a number. The number represents how many (0-2) old system badges need to be forfeited in order to get the new badge. High status people cannot cut in line. People who have questions cannot hold up the line. The major selling point is that the pre-cut badges are easier to get and if an individual takes at least two they may use your knife to put slits in their 'position sheets.'" (NOTE: Participants are not advised that this phase exists.)

## OBSERVATIONS/DEBRIEFING

The game takes approximately 30-45 minutes to complete with about 50 individuals. A minimum of one observer for every 5 participants allows for adequate coverage of the game floor. The observers record process and content of the various individuals, subgroups and change agent. From the beginning of the game, participants were competing for status by using their middle names, changed first names to become nicknames, etc., in order to get more badges. Persons at the table where the scissors were dull became agitated, some left and went to the other table, others became frustrated and crowded around the table to figure how to assist or "help themselves to the uncut pages with badges" (and then used a pocket knife, the pin in their name badge, etc.). Another problem that surfaced for the participants was that no provision was made for affixing the badges onto the 'position sheets,' however that didn't stop the participants from creating a whole range of options. Some neatly "dog eared" the badge to the sheet, other's cut slits into the sheets to slide in, others found tape lying around and procured it and others carried theirs around in their hand. The objective was to fill the 'position sheet' with badges; when the change agent is introduced many people were weary of the "blue" badges because the others were yellow. Those whose sheets were almost filled were loudly proclaiming that the "blue" badges were a fraud. Since no specific information was given, assumptions about color, how to place the badges on the sheet, etc. were varied. Participants were also observed to exhibit the following behaviors: giving up and dropping out, coalition building ("all win by helping one"), creating new norms, mistrusting of change agent, sabotaging the norms by hiding the scissors, using their own devices, and other types of deviant behavior (cheating, lying, stealing). The debriefing covers three points: (a) how the participants felt during the simulation: (b) what was the meaning of their behavior; and (c) identifying similar behaviors in "real life" social systems such as advantages of higher status, risk taking, resistance to change, "no win situations," etc. In this case, those with high status and one coalition member won the game.

## ADVANTAGES

The issue of racial/ethnic dynamics is "backed" into by looking at have's and have-not's, social systems and social change. Concepts such as unfair biases in the old system and forfeitures in the new system may result in "some people just cannot get ahead no matter how hard they try." This simulation allows each participant to analyze his/her own behavior given a particular status and extrapolate that into understanding why others may behave the way they do in "real social system."

## POSSIBLE MODIFICATIONS

The concept of winning was adequate motivation for most participants, in actuality there was no gift. What would have been the dynamics if a television or jewelry were announced at the beginning? Instead of assigning status by name, use racial, ethnic identity; those having the more multicultural experience (personal or experiential) get more badges. Increase the benefits for making a change, e.g., special gifts.